AF265889

MONSTERS

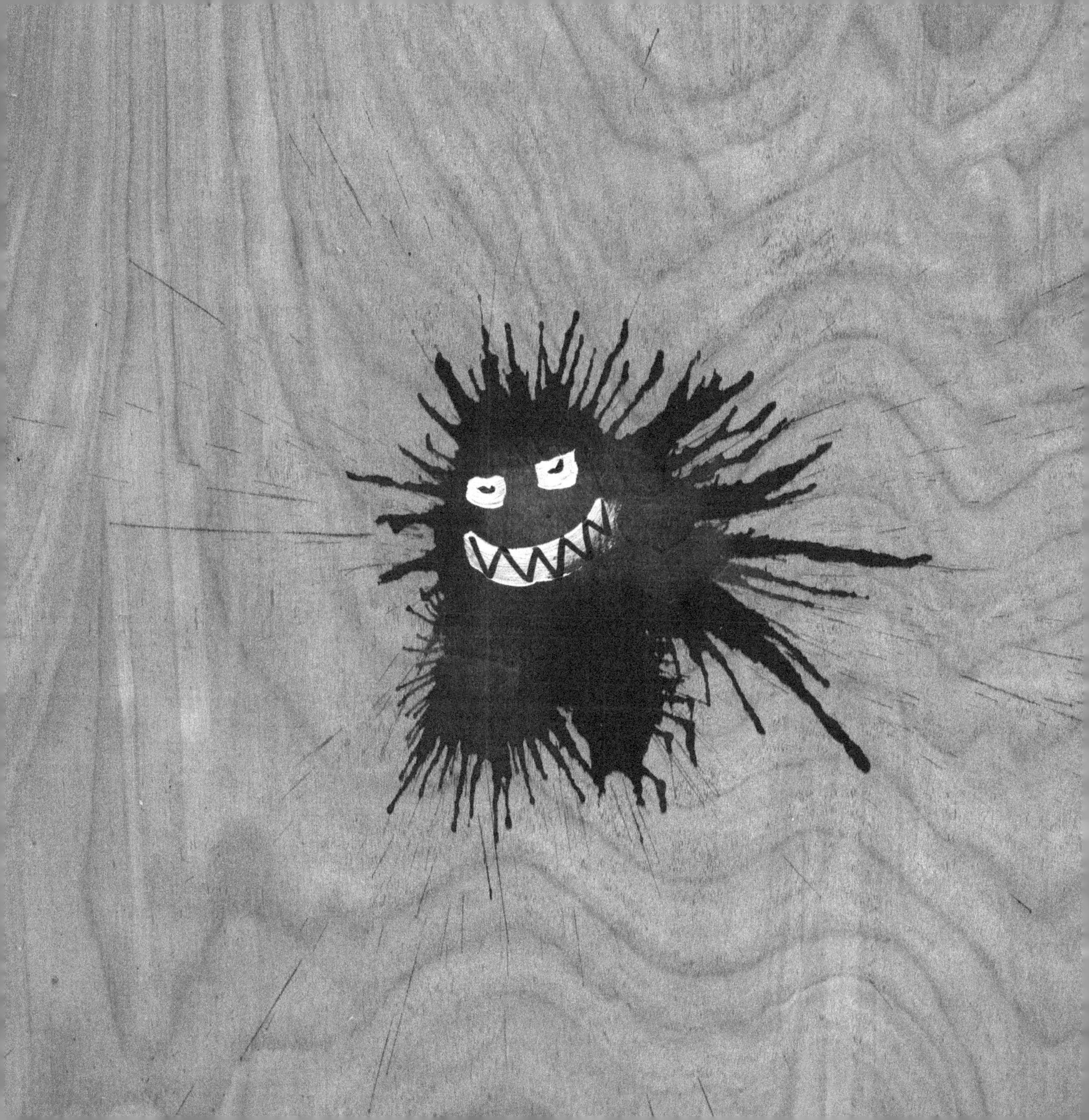

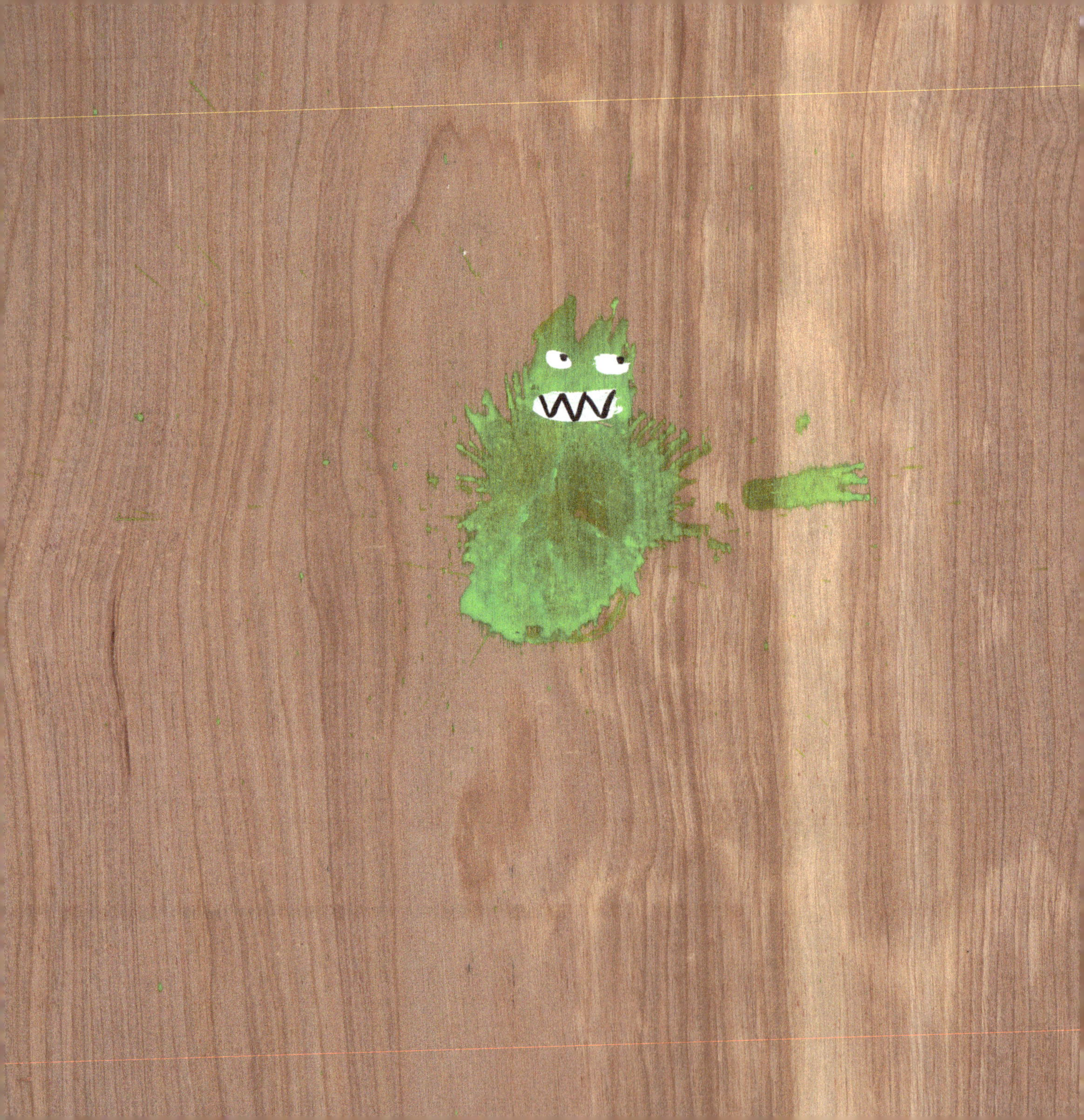

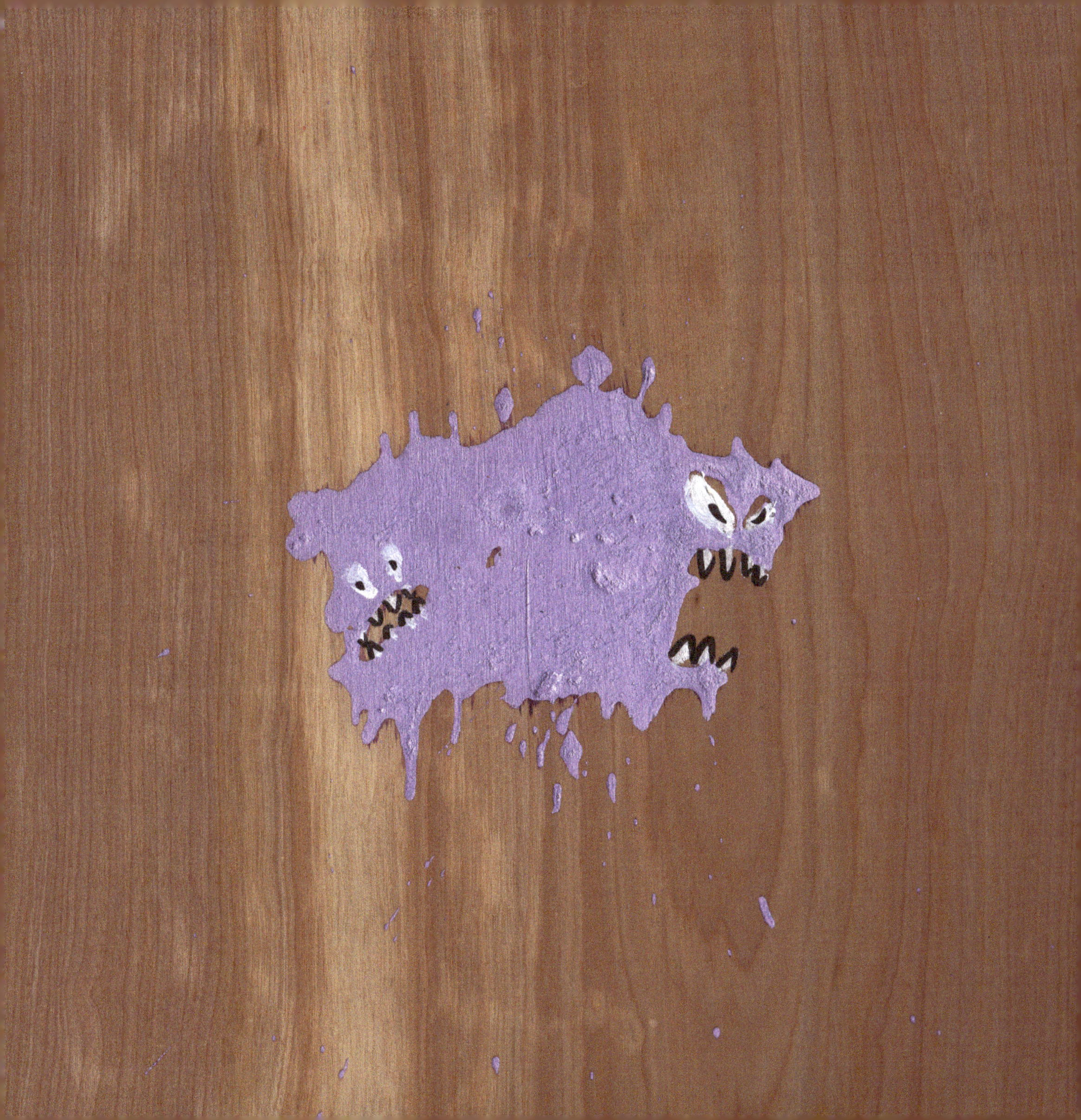

MONSTERS

Being a Poem and Paintings by

PACA
LAVARA

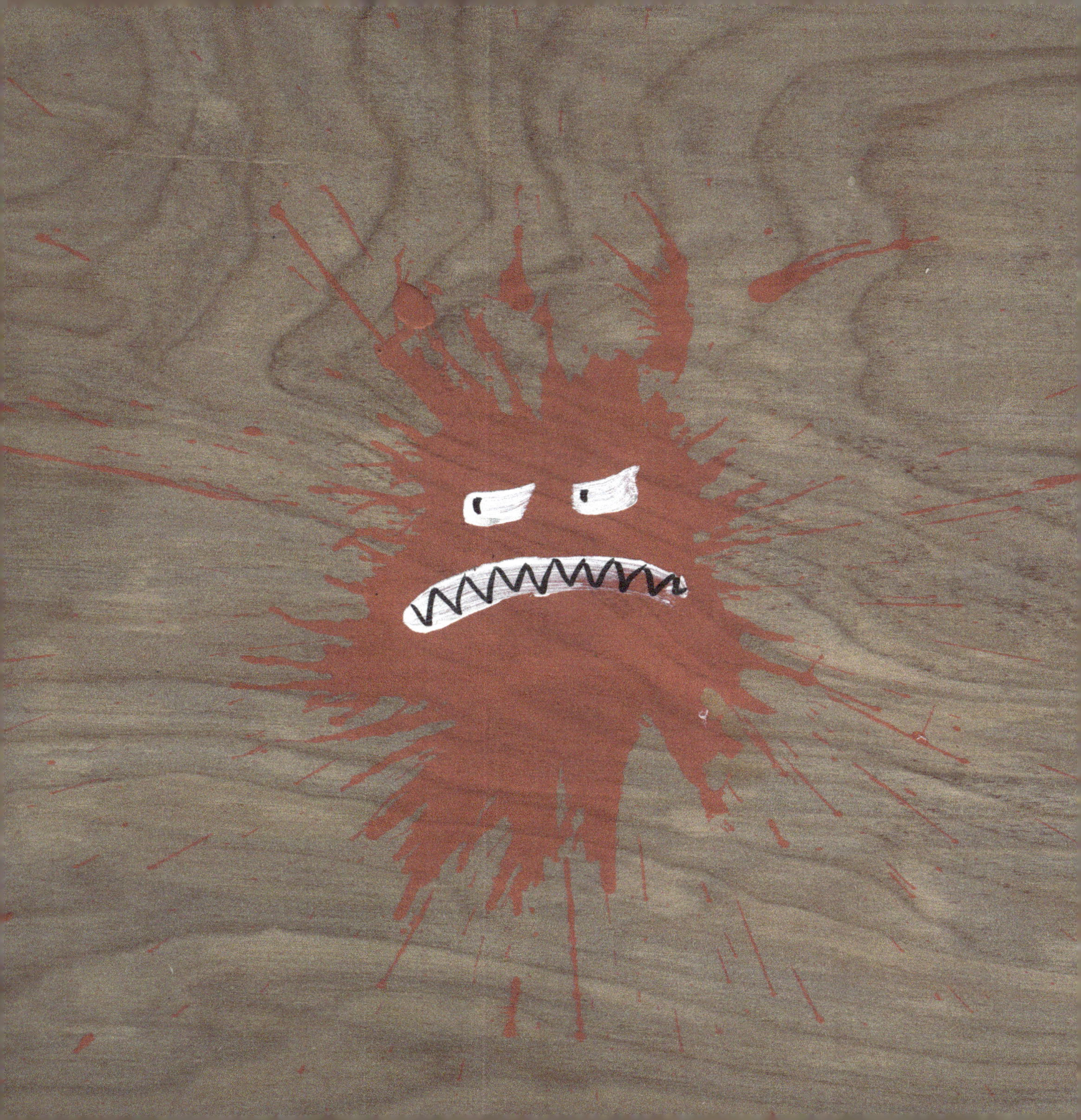

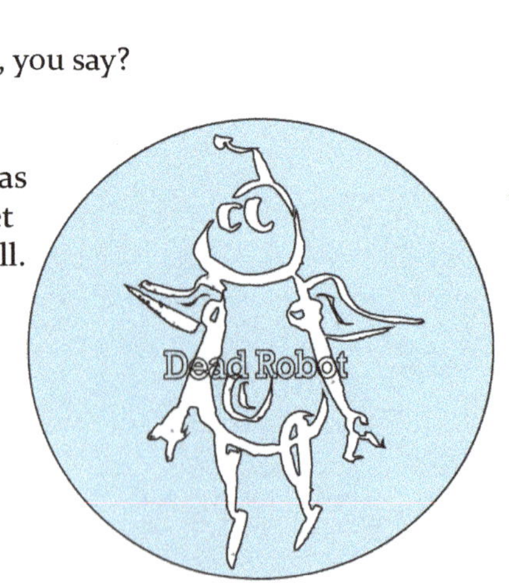
Dead Robot

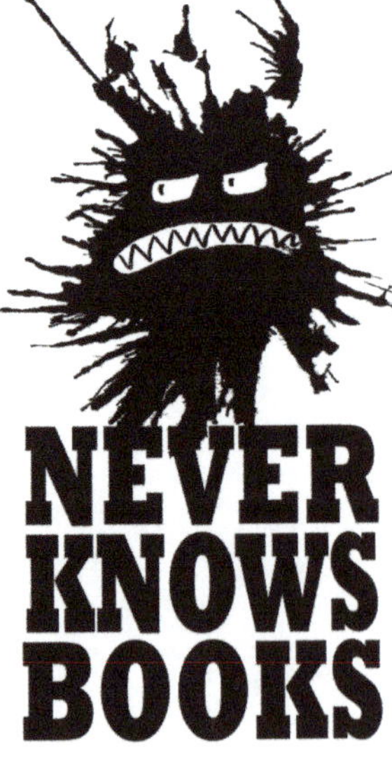
NEVER
KNOWS
BOOKS

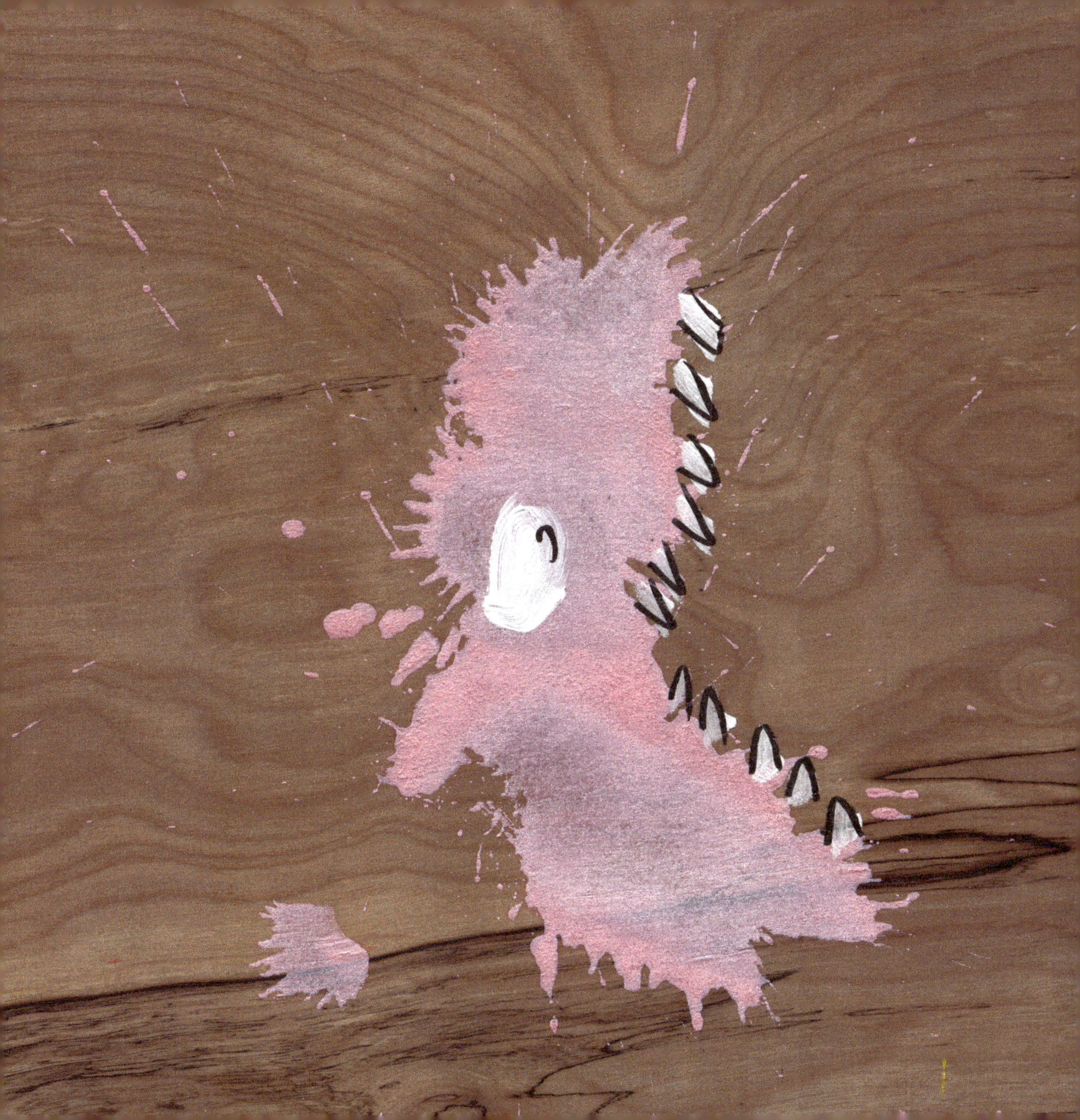

Dedicated

to

Edward Lear

...

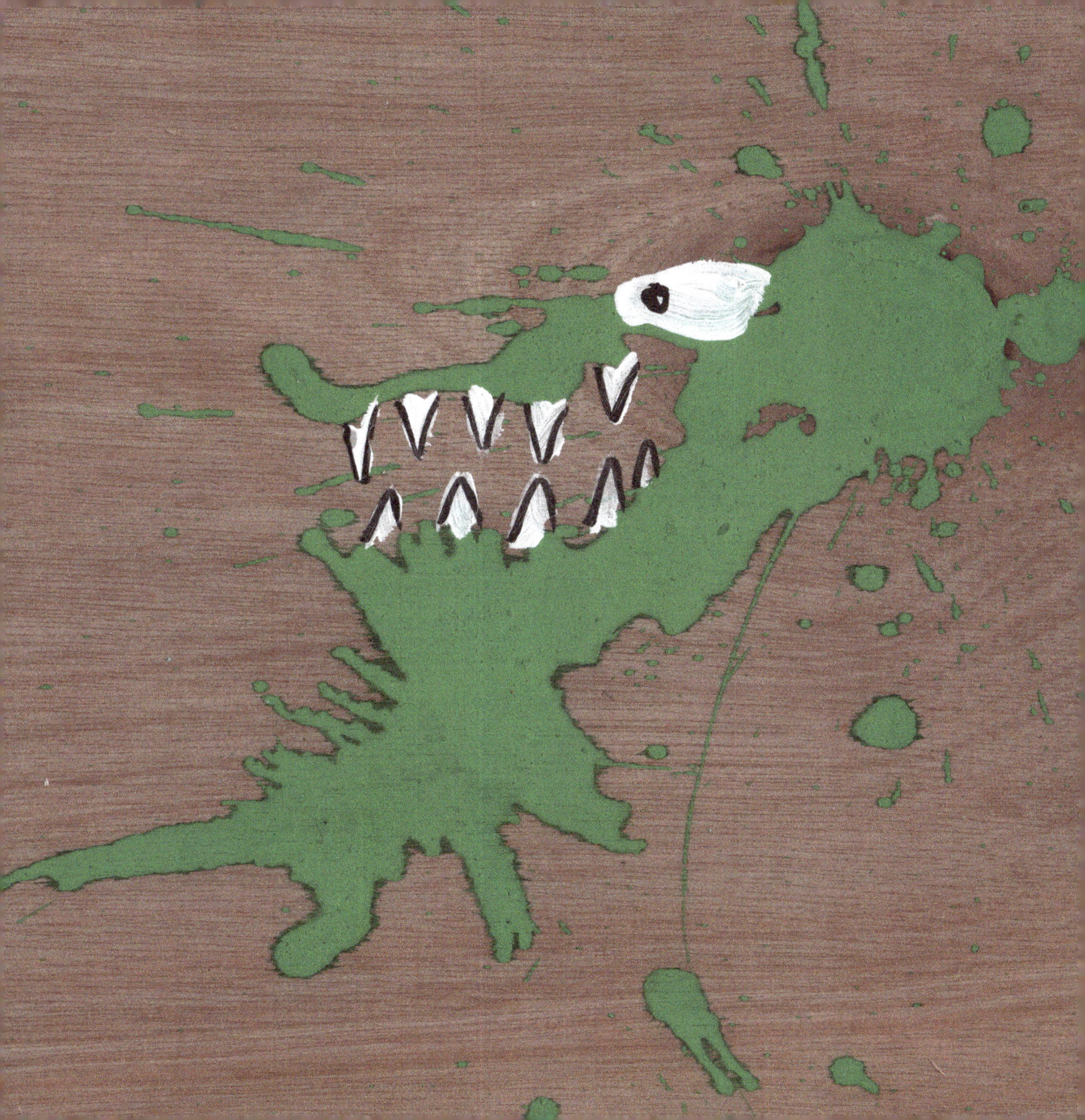

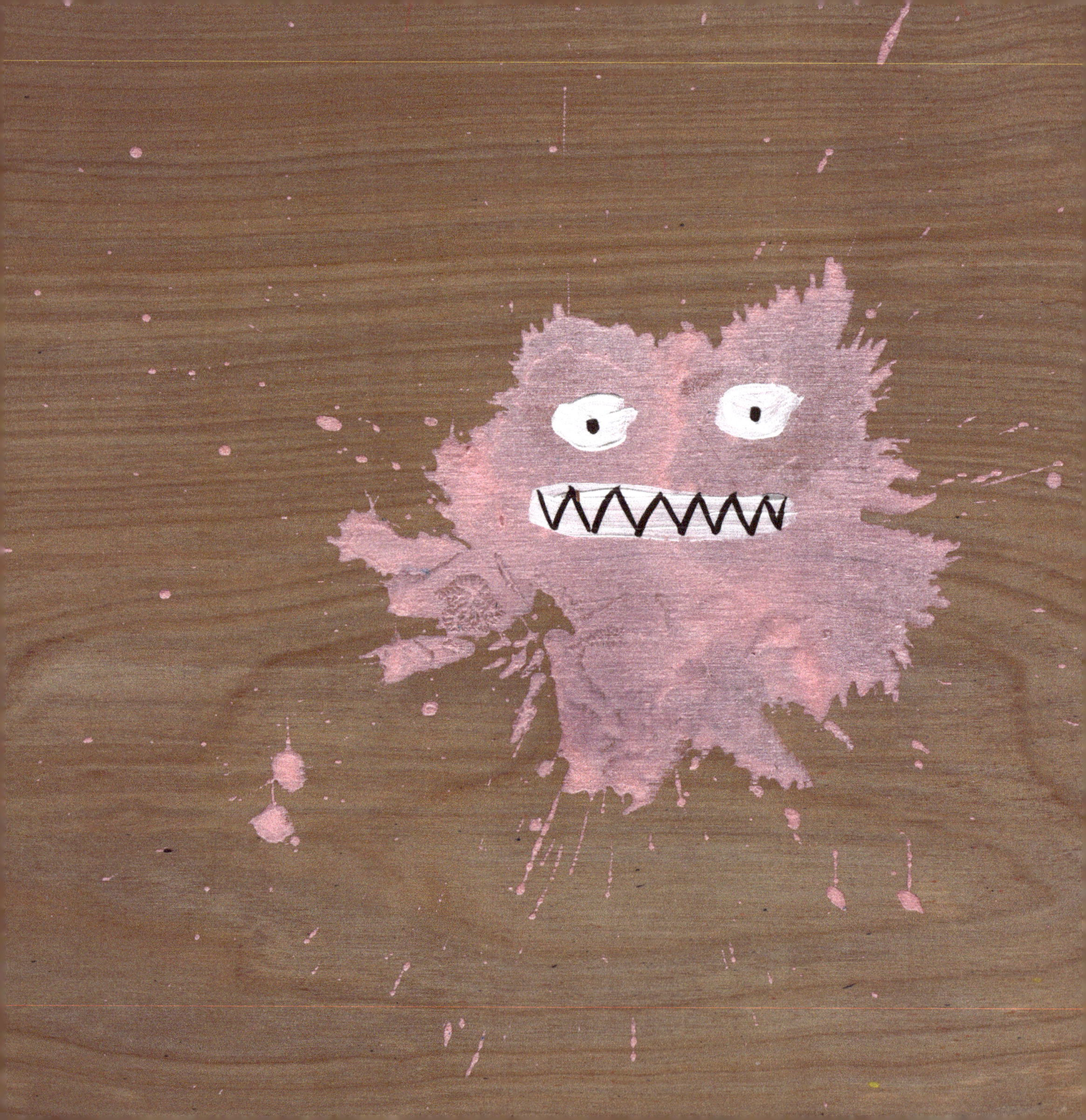

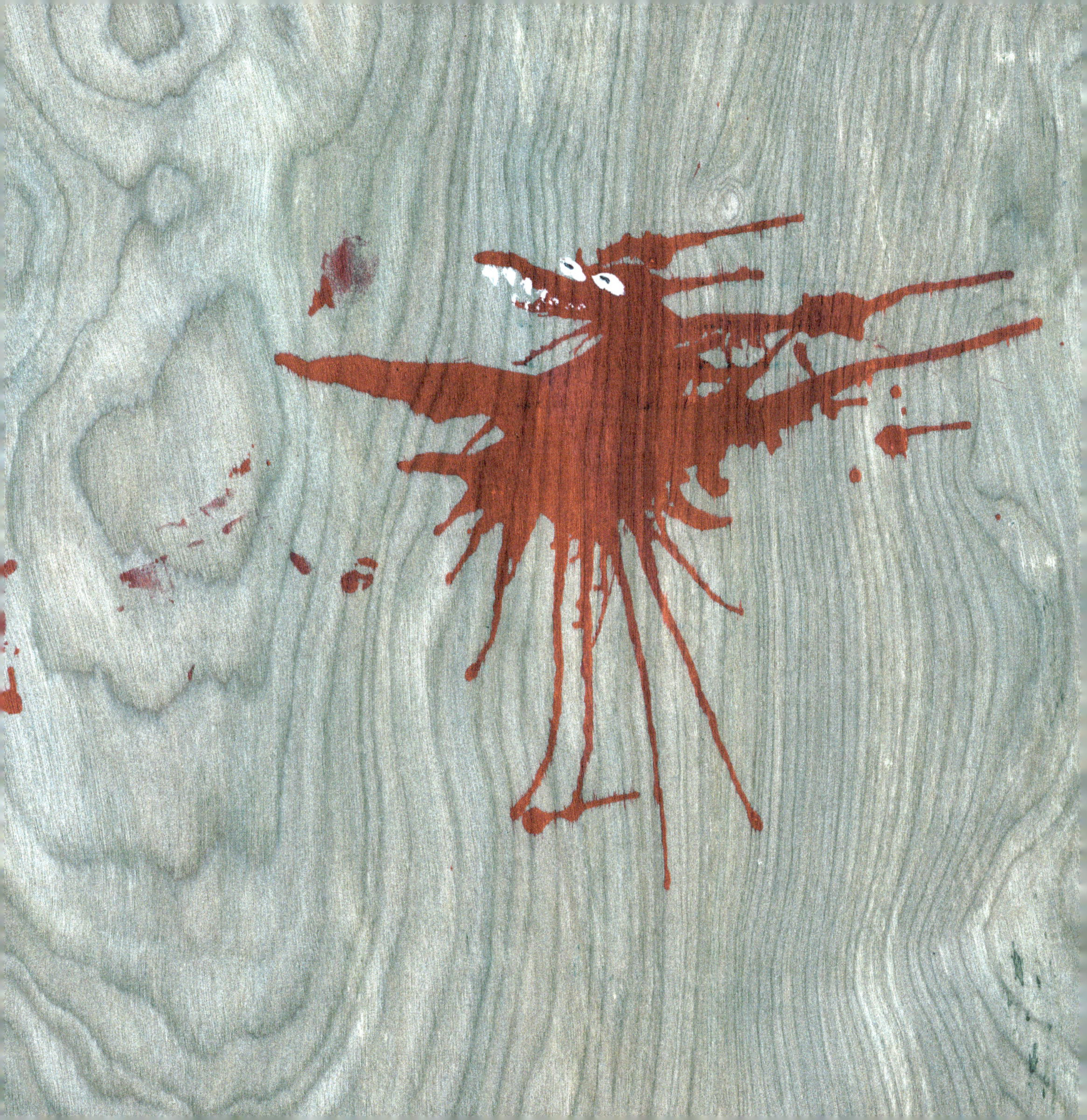

All together now gather
You monsters, misanthropes, and men
Hark to nothing, slide, and then
Ambrosia settles in for peaceful slumber
Animals
While allegory has your number
But will it ever—
And you wait there for the phone to ring
All together, shout it out: sing
All together, shout it to the sky

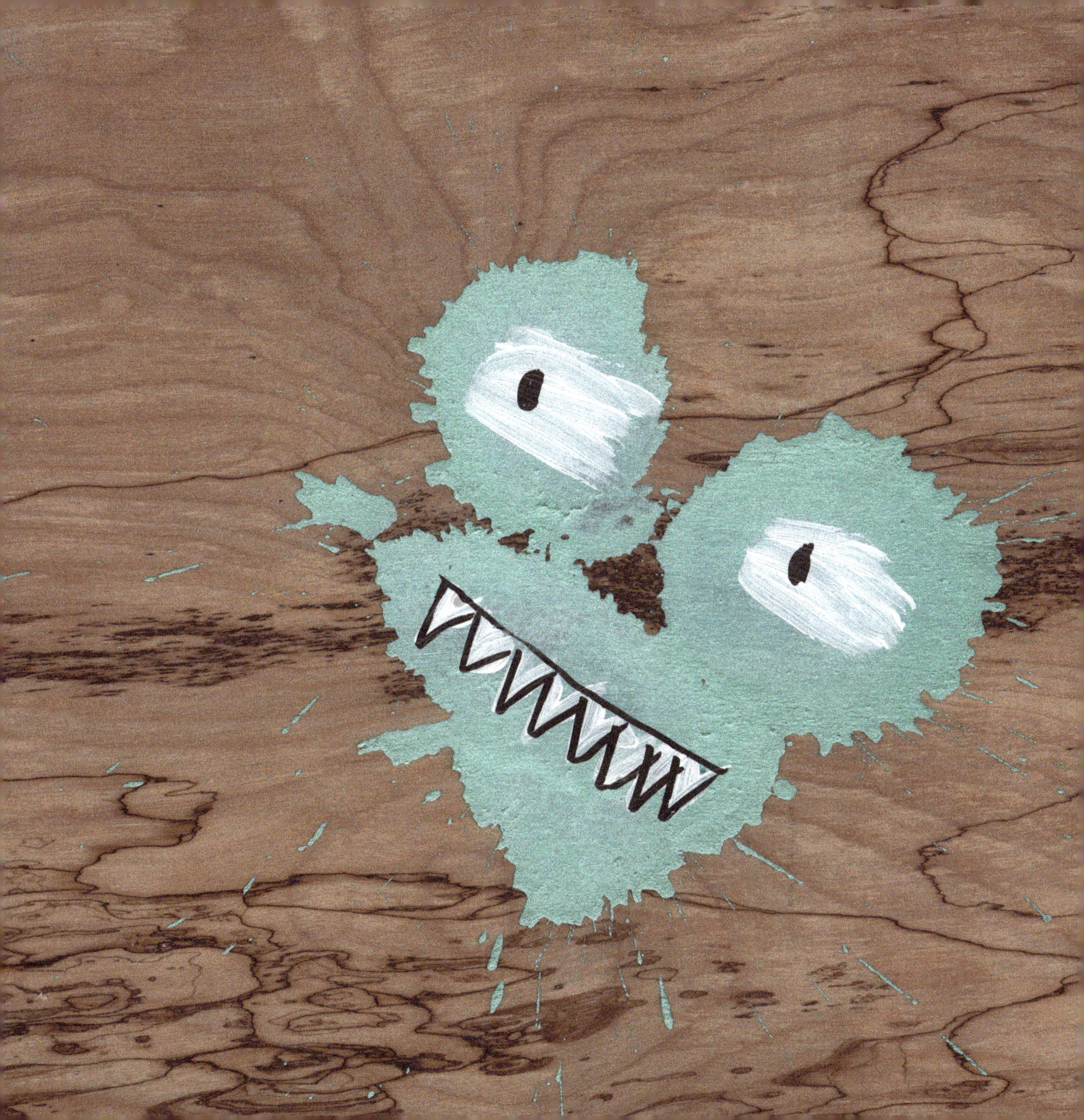

Bombast!
But man those bellicose bastards ride high

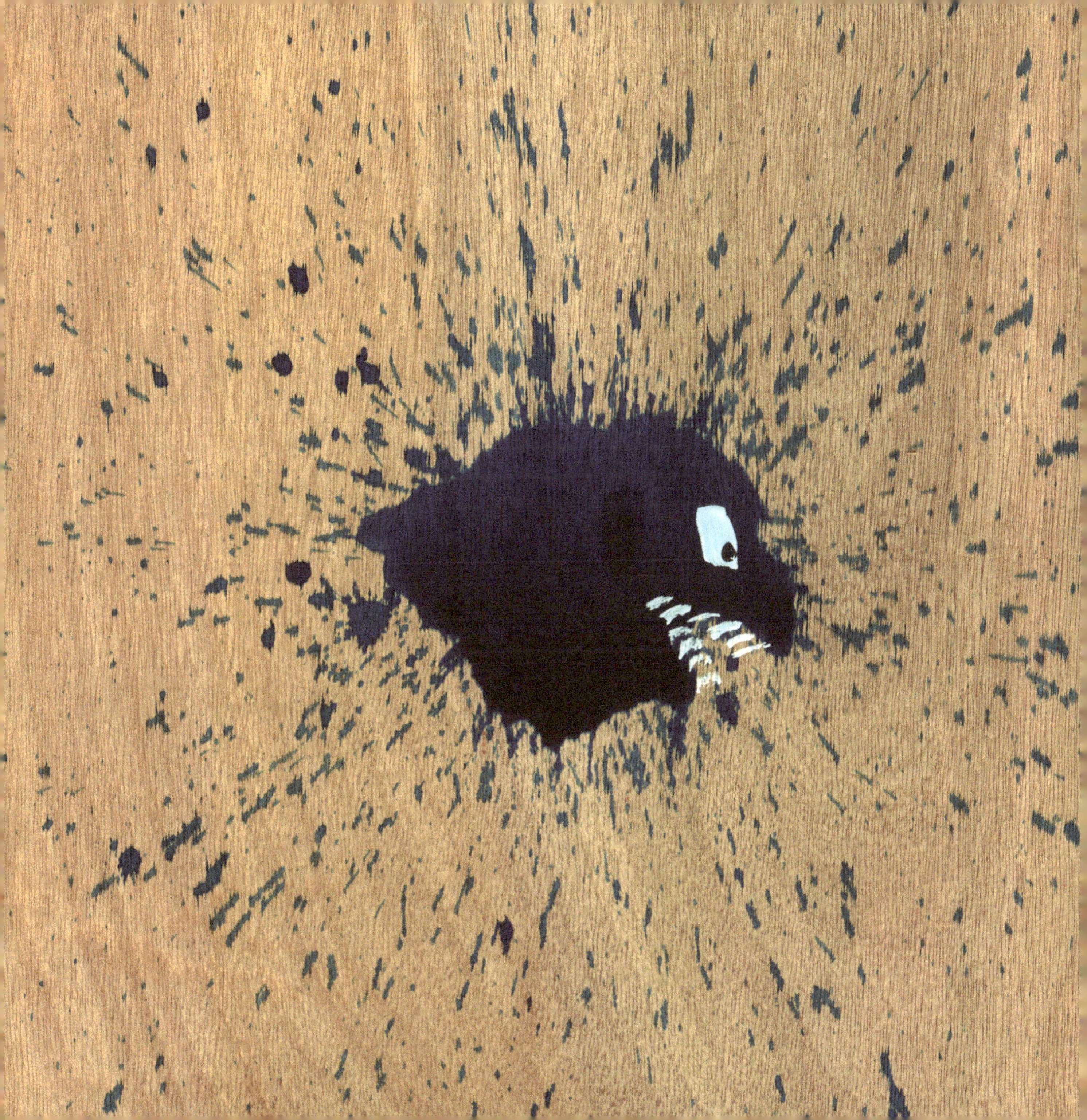

Cut your teeth and sharpen your horns,
Claws, and spindly wings and things
You wore kept shorn.
Cue the citizens and
Cling to them to bring them down
Cling to me— let's drown.

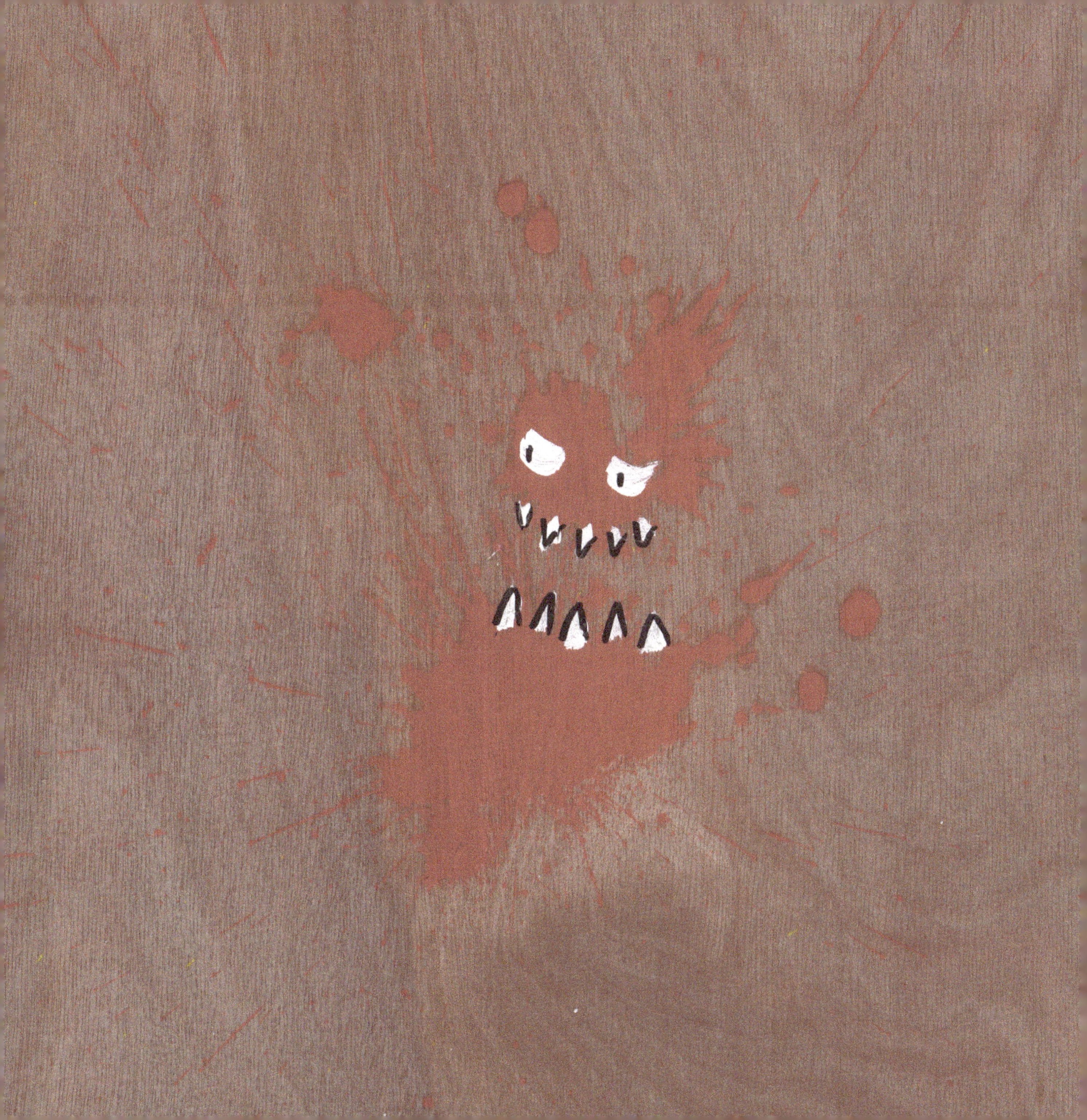

Destruction comes with not a sound
Crumpled masks litter the ground
Dead? Not I not us not yet not we nor me
He never saw the sea
How tragic.
How cliche
Doom never comes to those who wait
And watched pots never say.

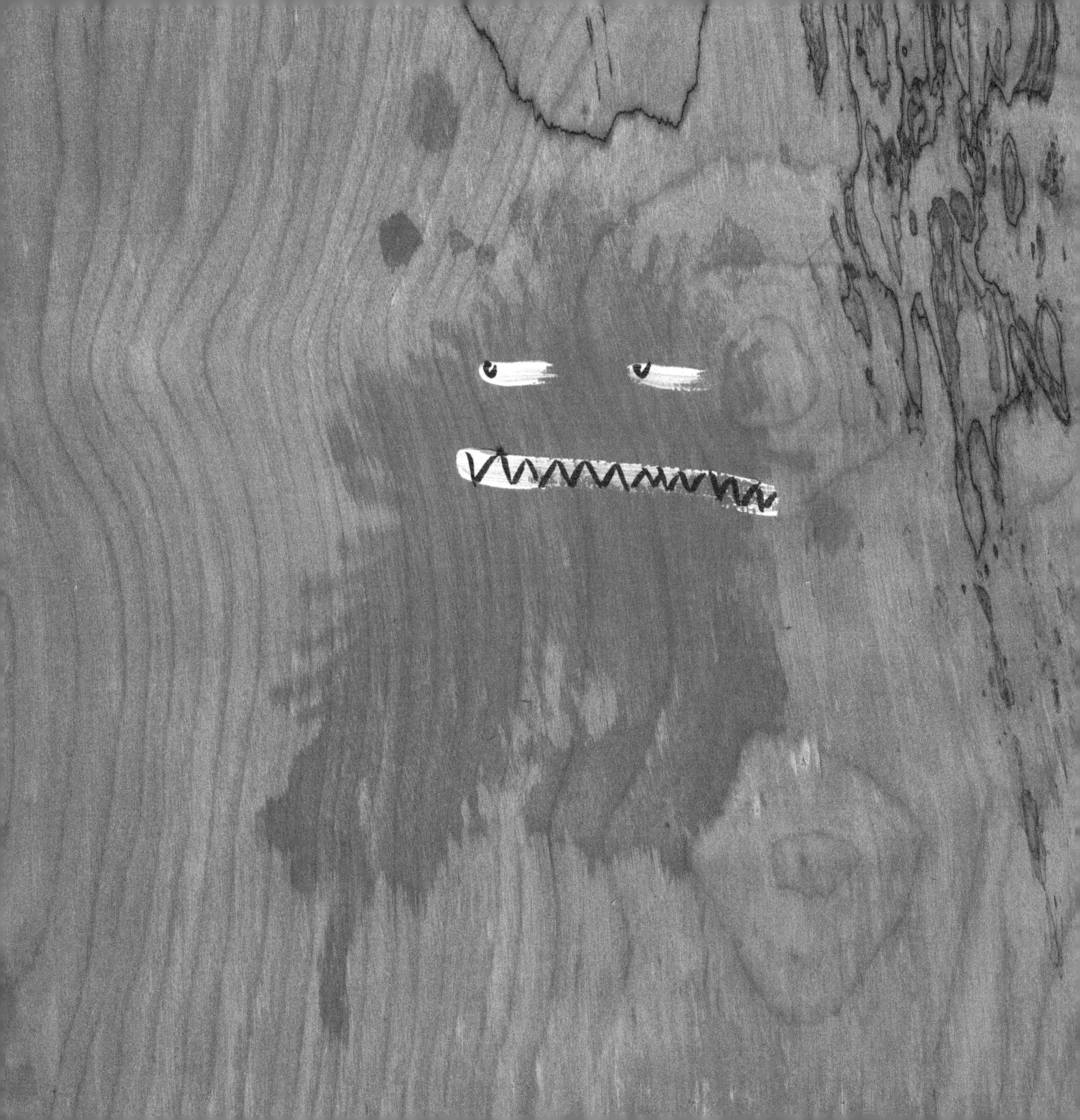

Everyone rattles sabers at the
New monsters now and then
As they emerge to put to test
What everyone says:
Only monsters and Monkey are headed out west.
Enemies cluster at the gates
Let's find a way to turn a tidy sum:
Everybody profit
From unchecked hate as
Empires are want to do
And Monsters, too

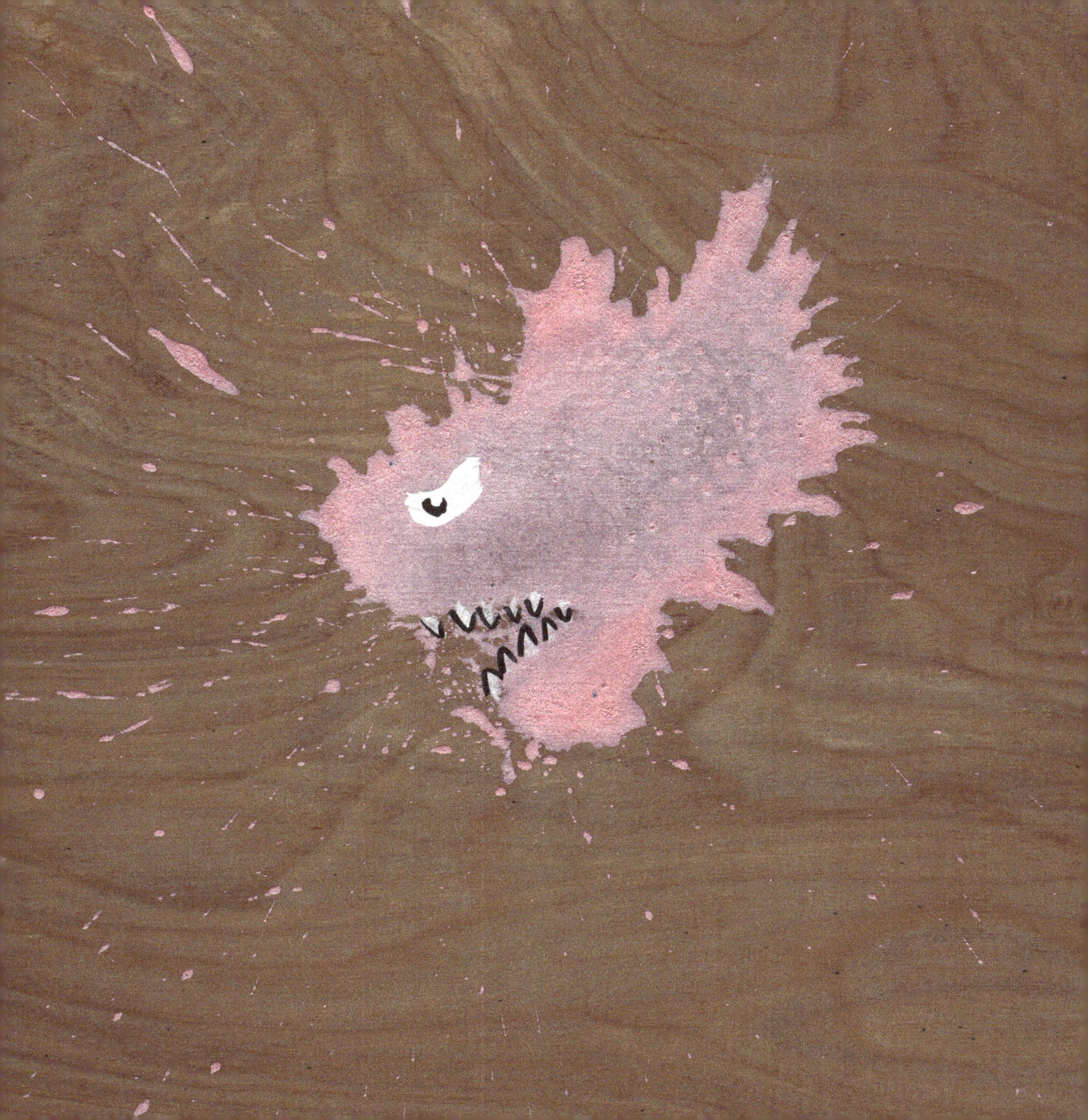

Fortune's favor held her hand
We fell to it because it was better than
Feeling sorry for... ellipses.
Fire held my belly
But something held her gaze

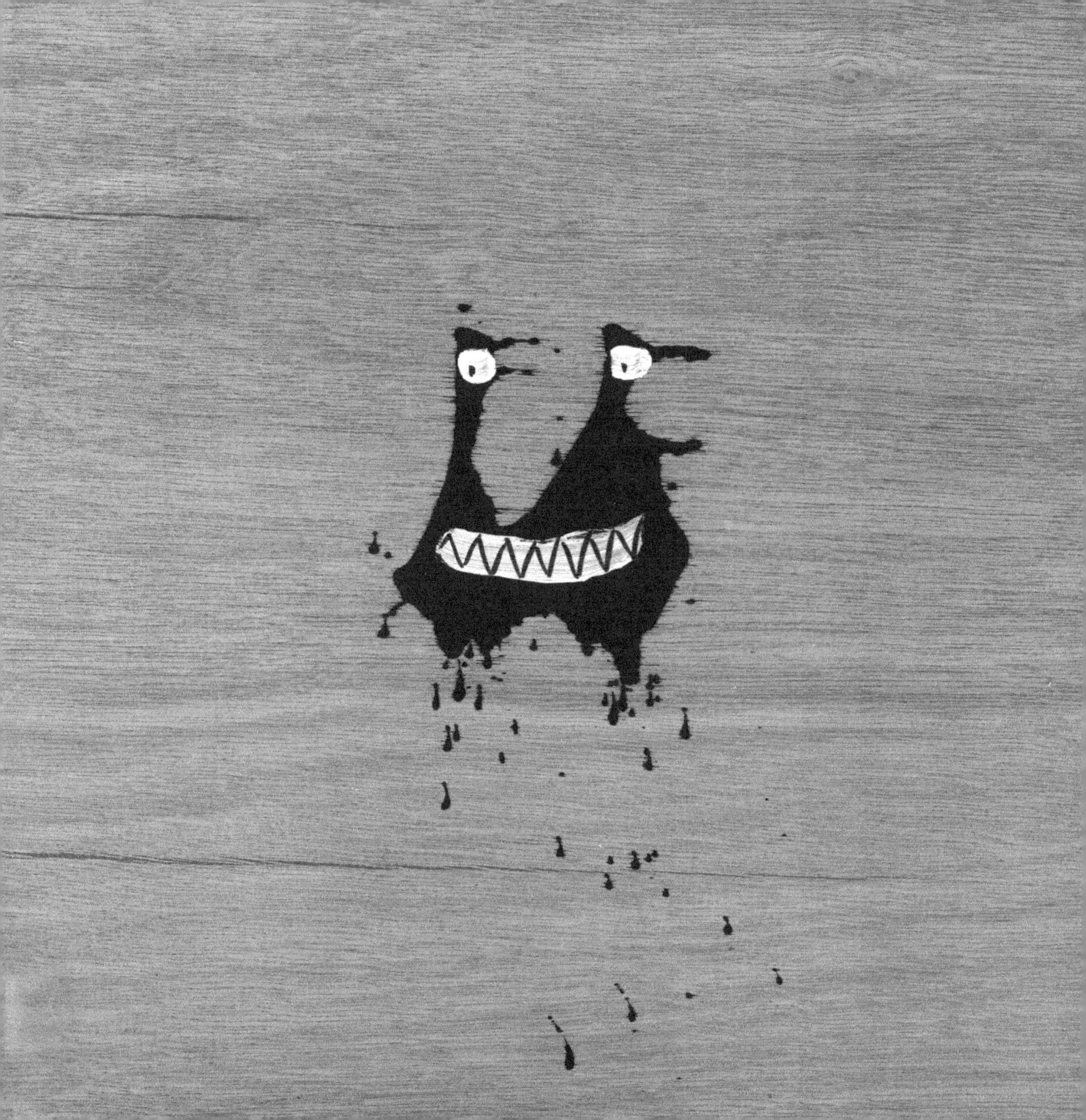

Gasping Groping all get out
There's nothing
In the middle of this maze.
All and...
Everybody down down down

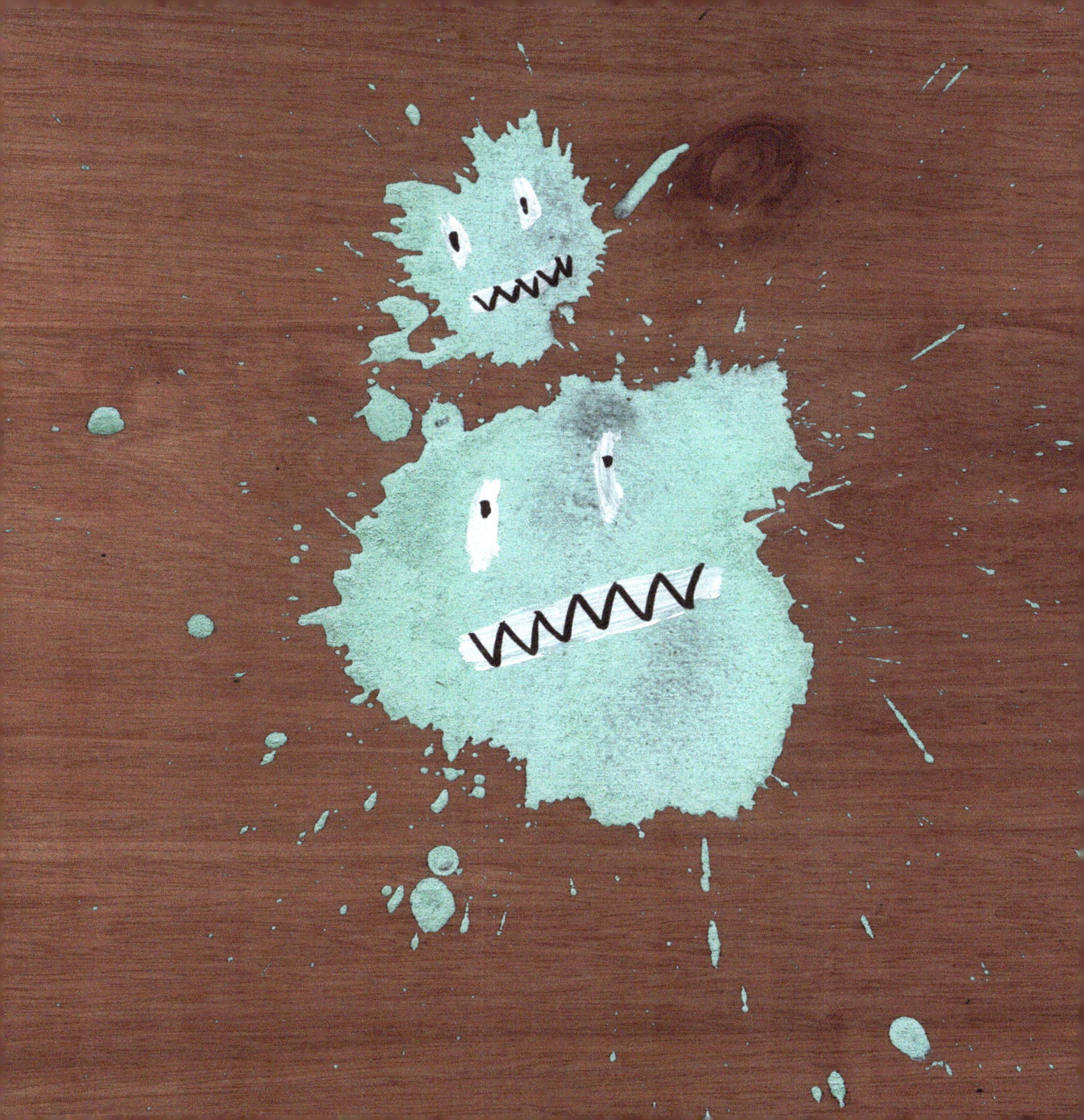

Heaven is a little slice of Heaven
And horns won't hold them back

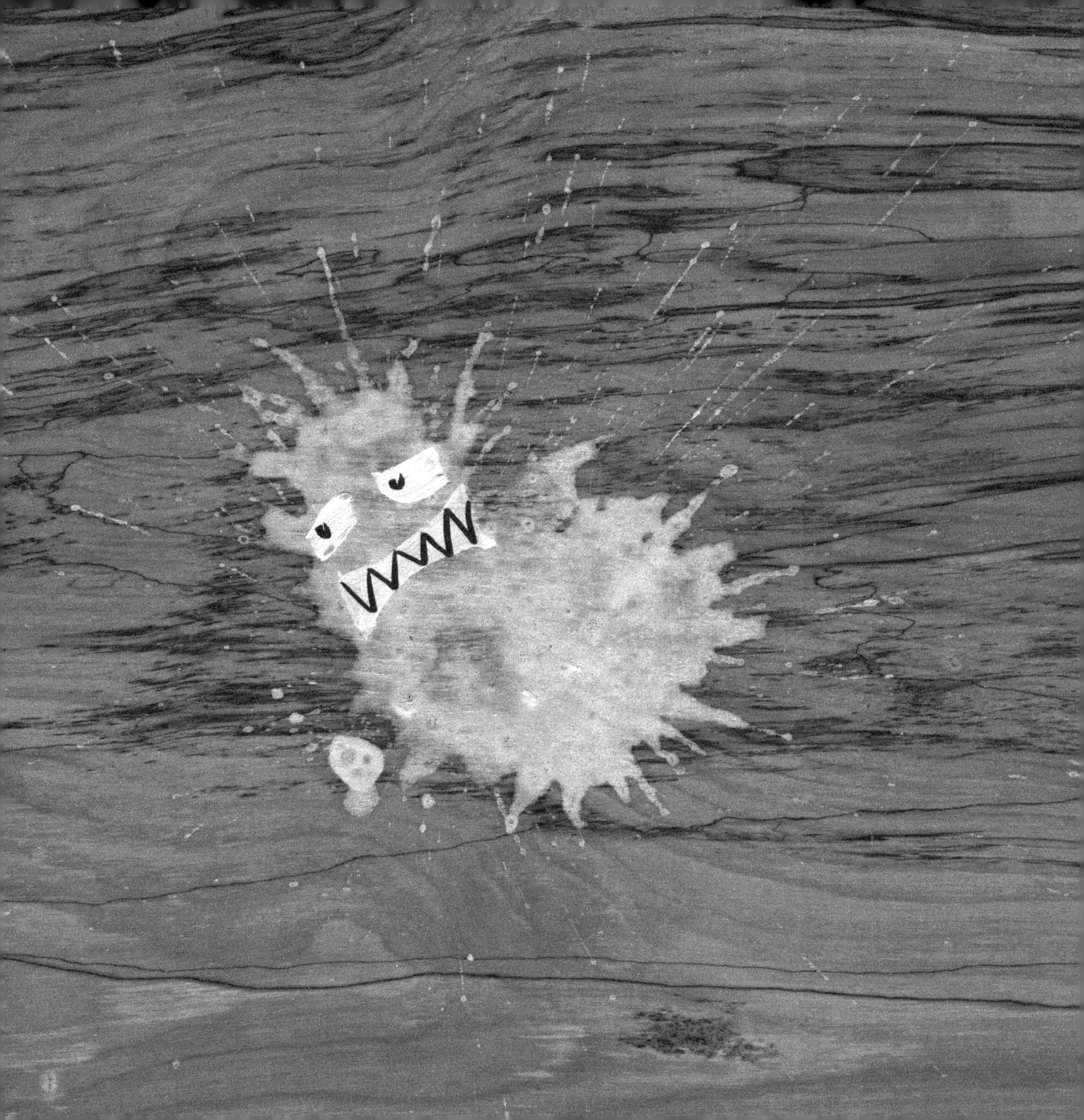

Is that really all it takes
To decry those things they lack?
Like food security and a warm bed
And a call to arms
Or whatever passes for will these days.
Iron.
Forged in blood or blood money
I'll stab it in
But monsters only win
What else is there to play?

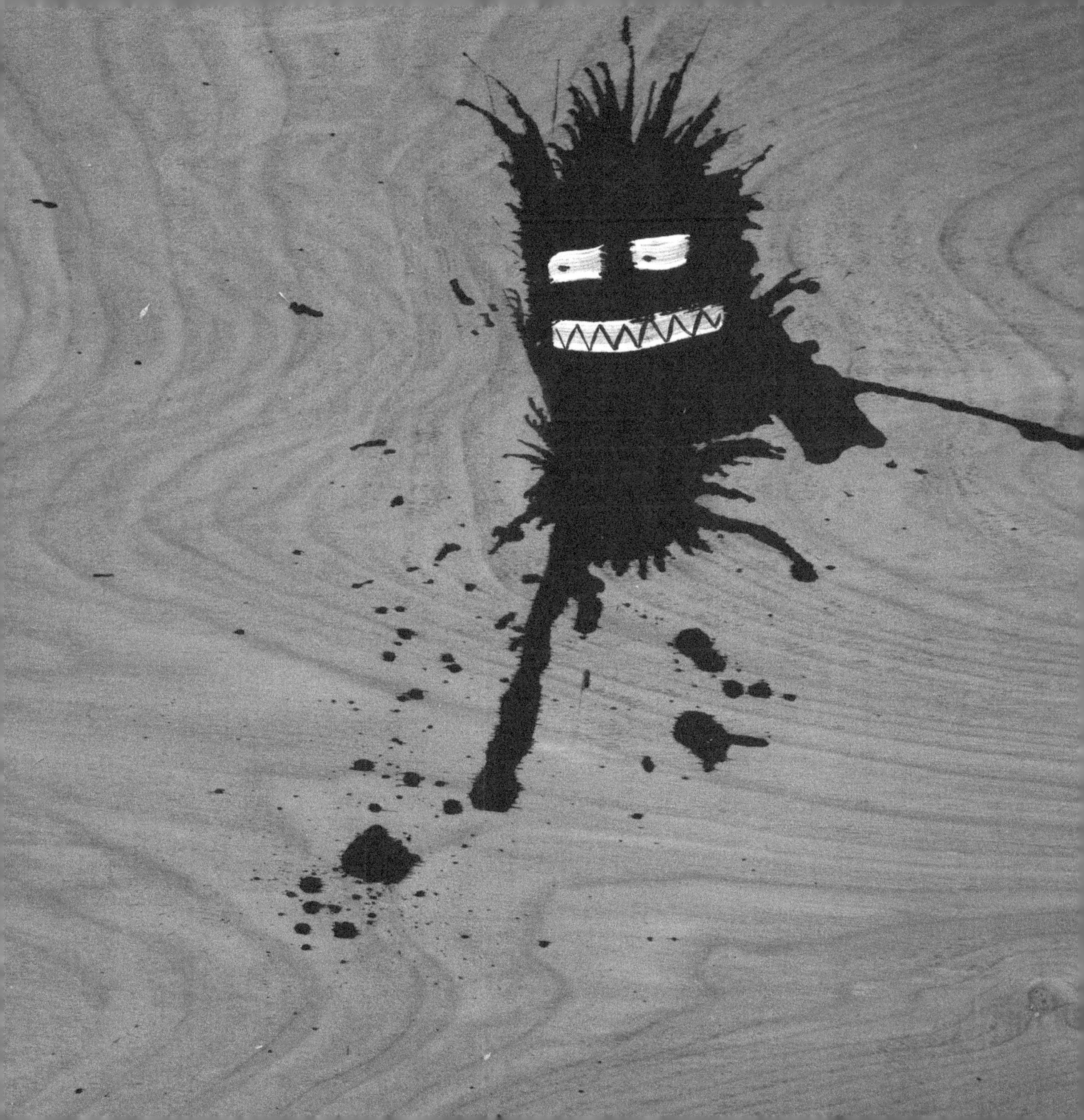

Justifications are easy here, or so they say
Now take it home
And teach the beasts to sway
Jump back, attack
Jet set, better than

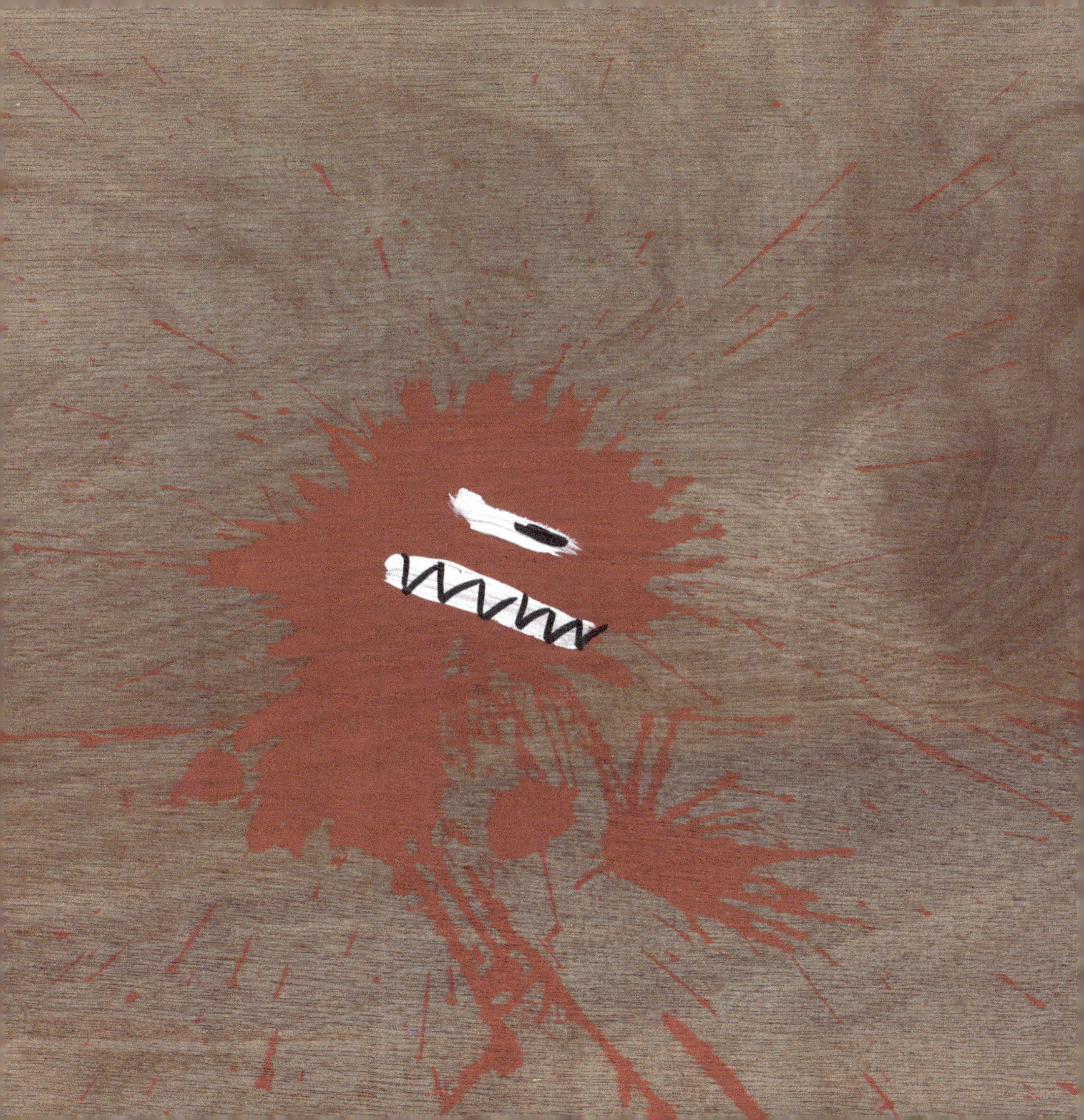

Kissing
Killing
Collisions
Thrilling
Sexed up lies lies lies

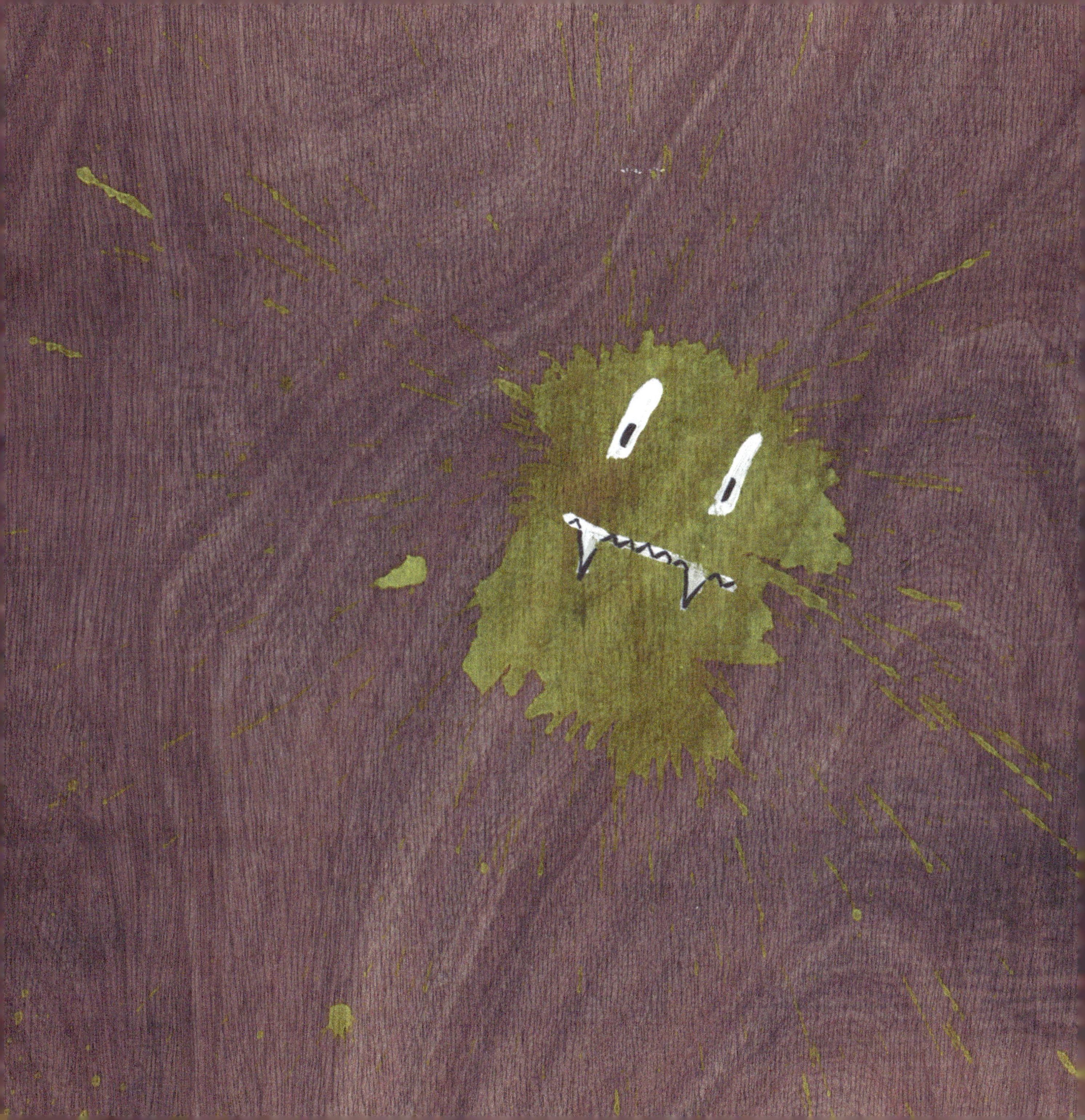

Lies lies.
Laying down together in a pile
Of worn out welcomes
That the animal kingdom
Traded for a song to see
Lusus Naturae. Latin. For

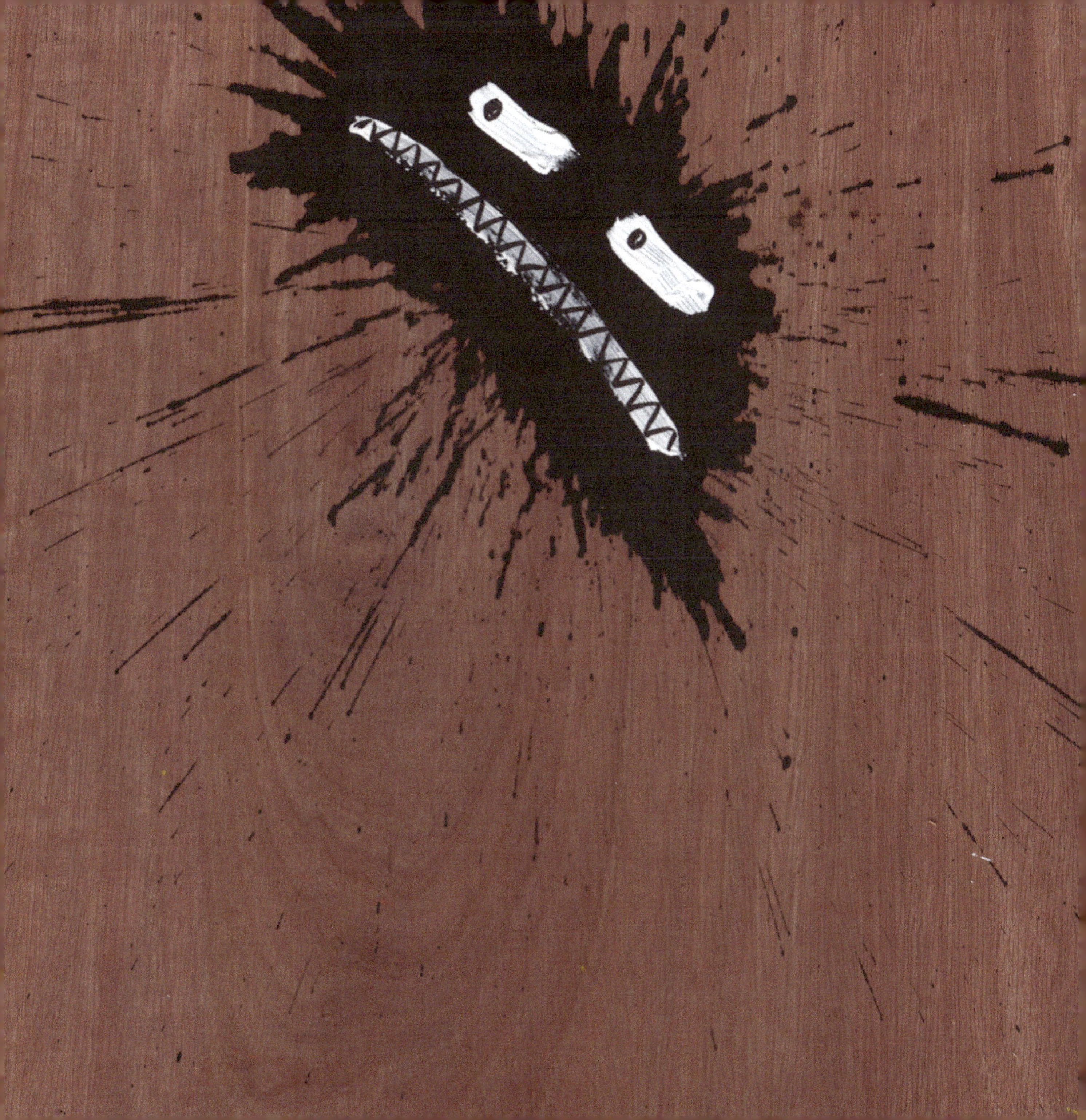

Monsters, misanthropes, and men and me
What do they say?
I hate all Montagues and thee?
Or something like that.

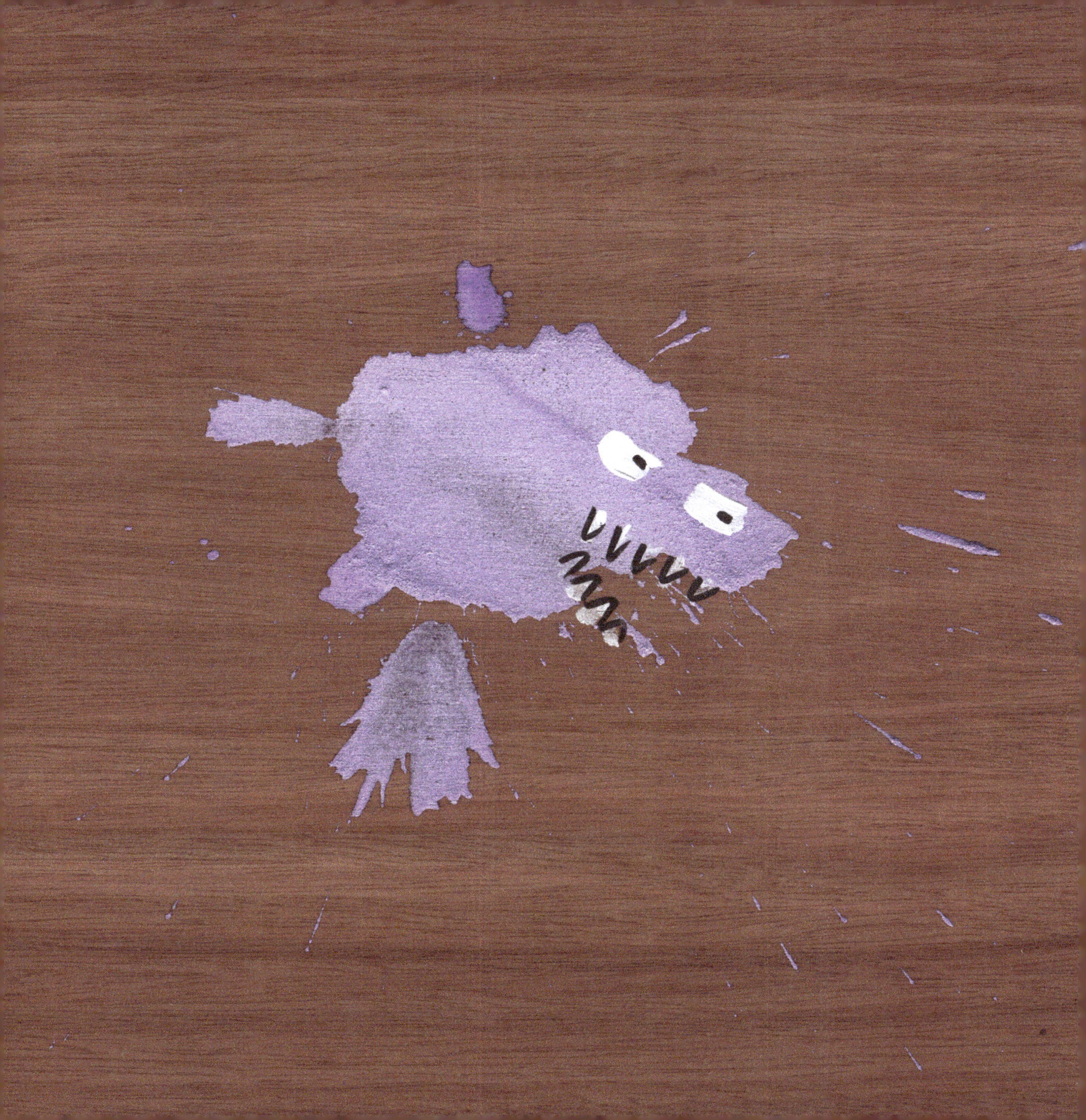

Never before have I better understood
So clearly what we know... Nevermind.
Nearly there, halfway
Did you never think to pray?
Naw.
...Nevermind.
Where did this sprout spring from anyways?
It's almost like...

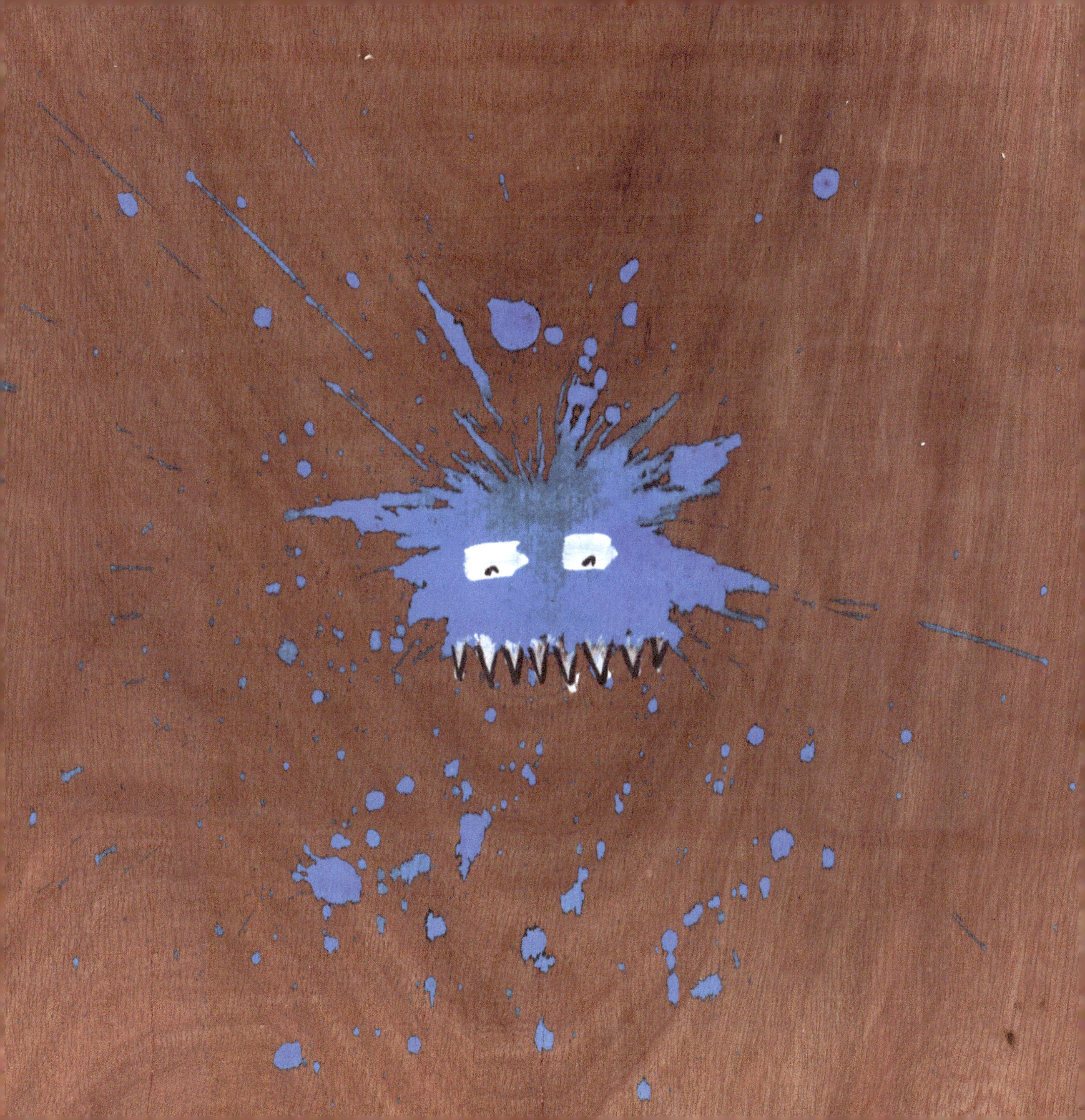

Origins:
Octopus and owl shacked up together
'Cuz tentacles, they say, do make it better
Or at least something different from
Status quo for awhile
Origins:
Gave a biblical birth to this

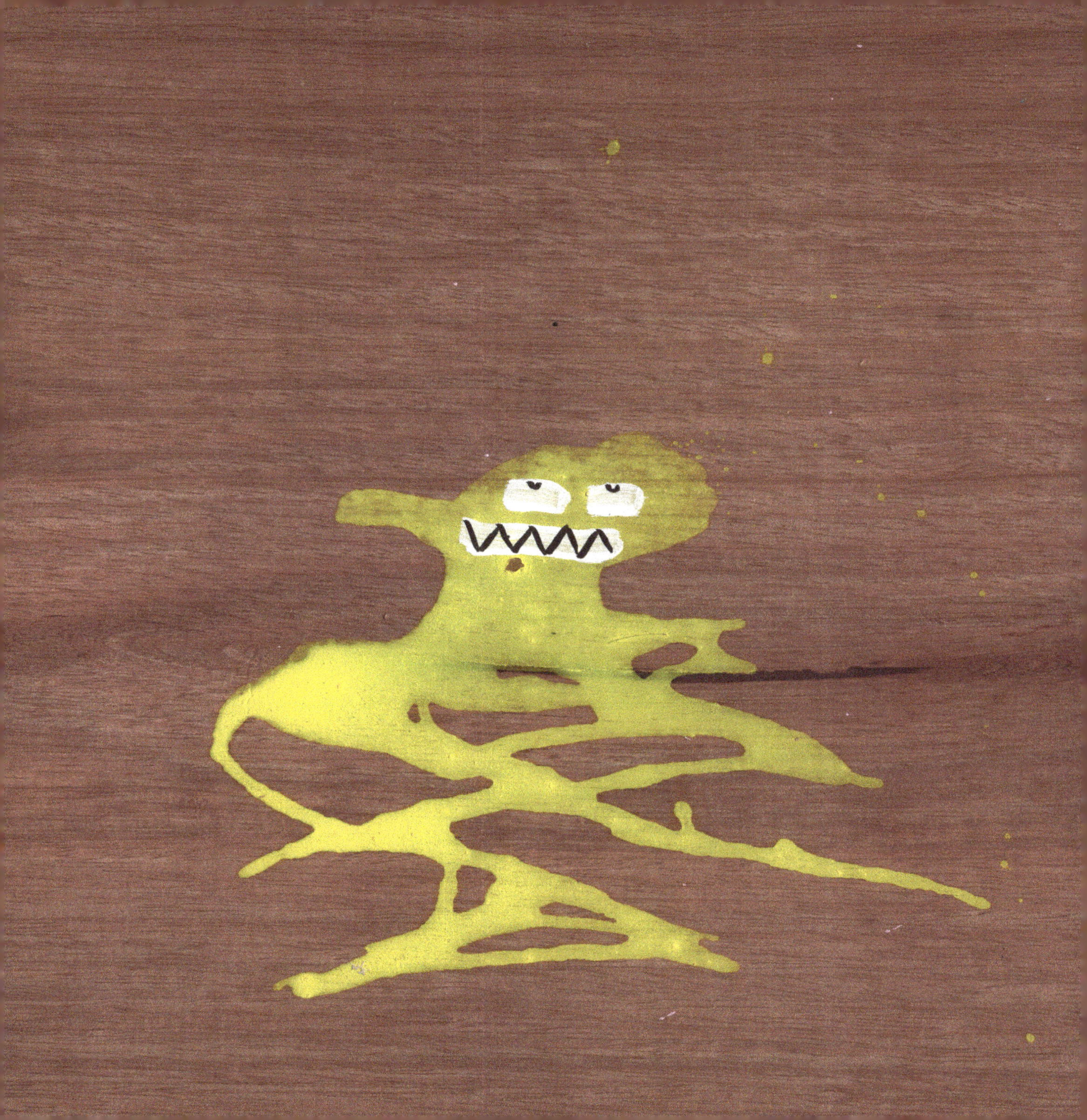

Progeny of misspent youth that
Falls to me like deja vu to
Pacify the proles and peds and
Parables you took to bed
And parasites inside your head
That priests and politicians said
Were silly little dreams
Profit motives to make men scream

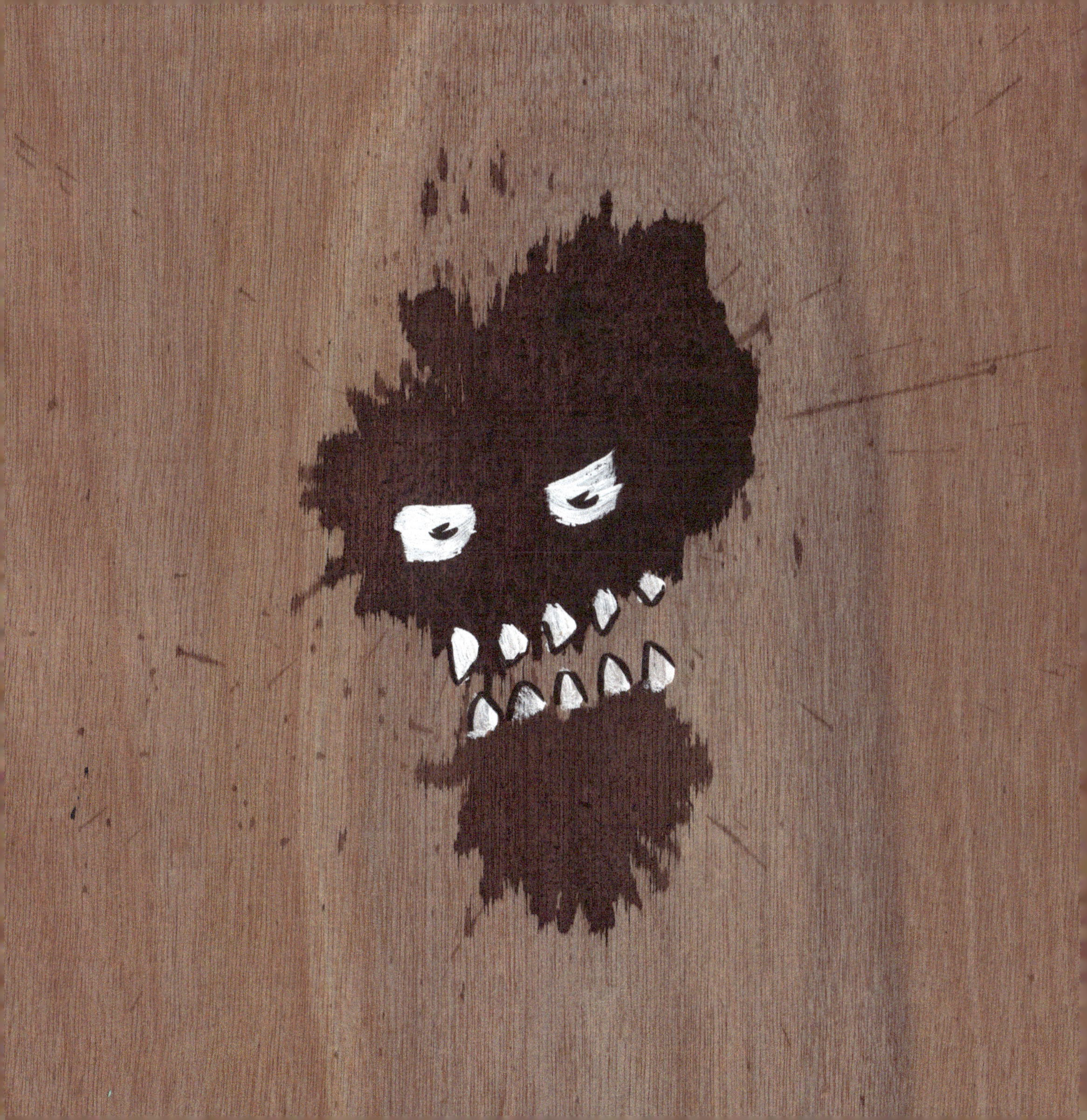

Queen me.

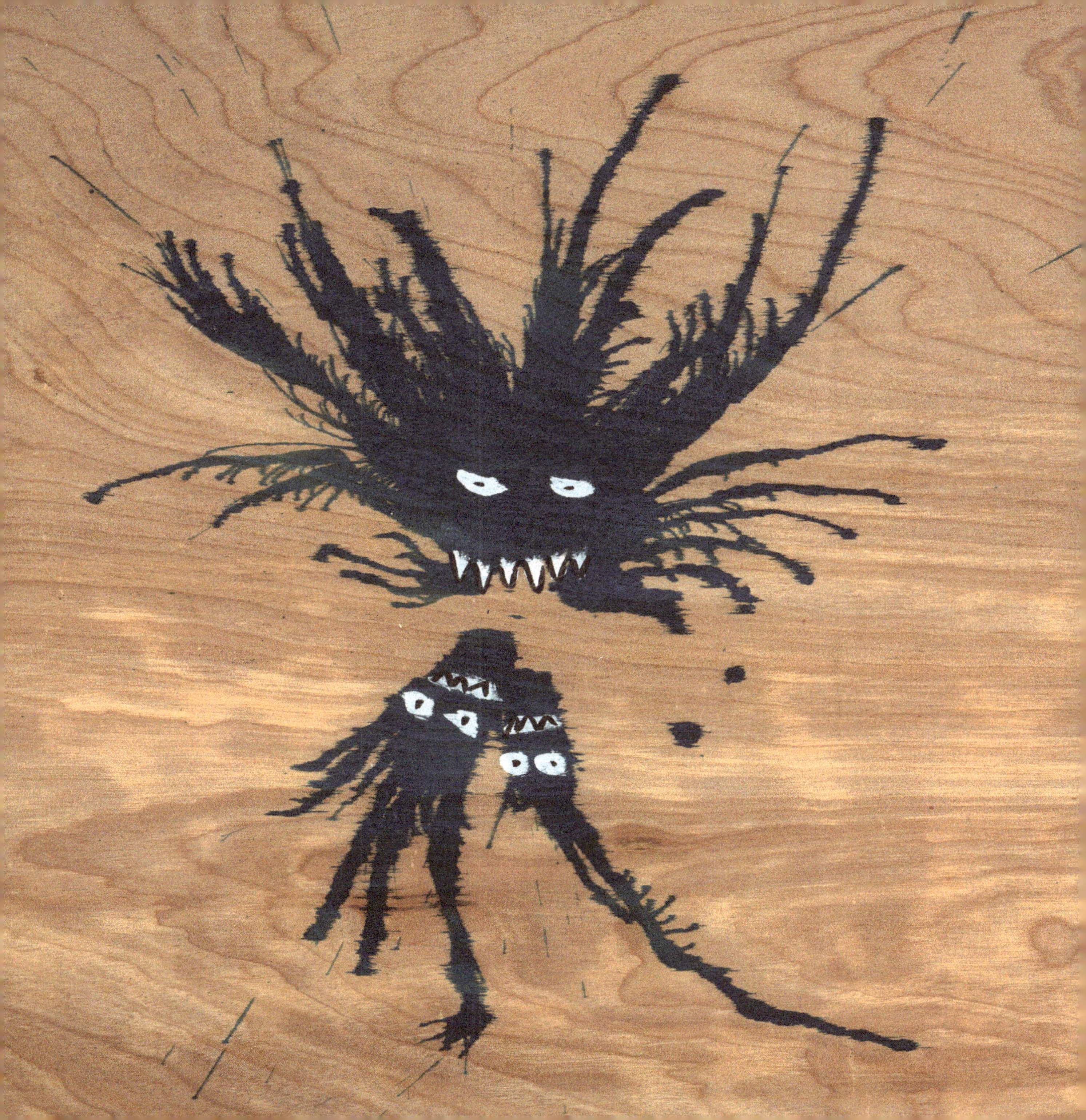

Rapacious appetite made glorious dawn
By sharpened tooth and bloody claw
Before the battle lines were drawn
And sucked into their gaping maw

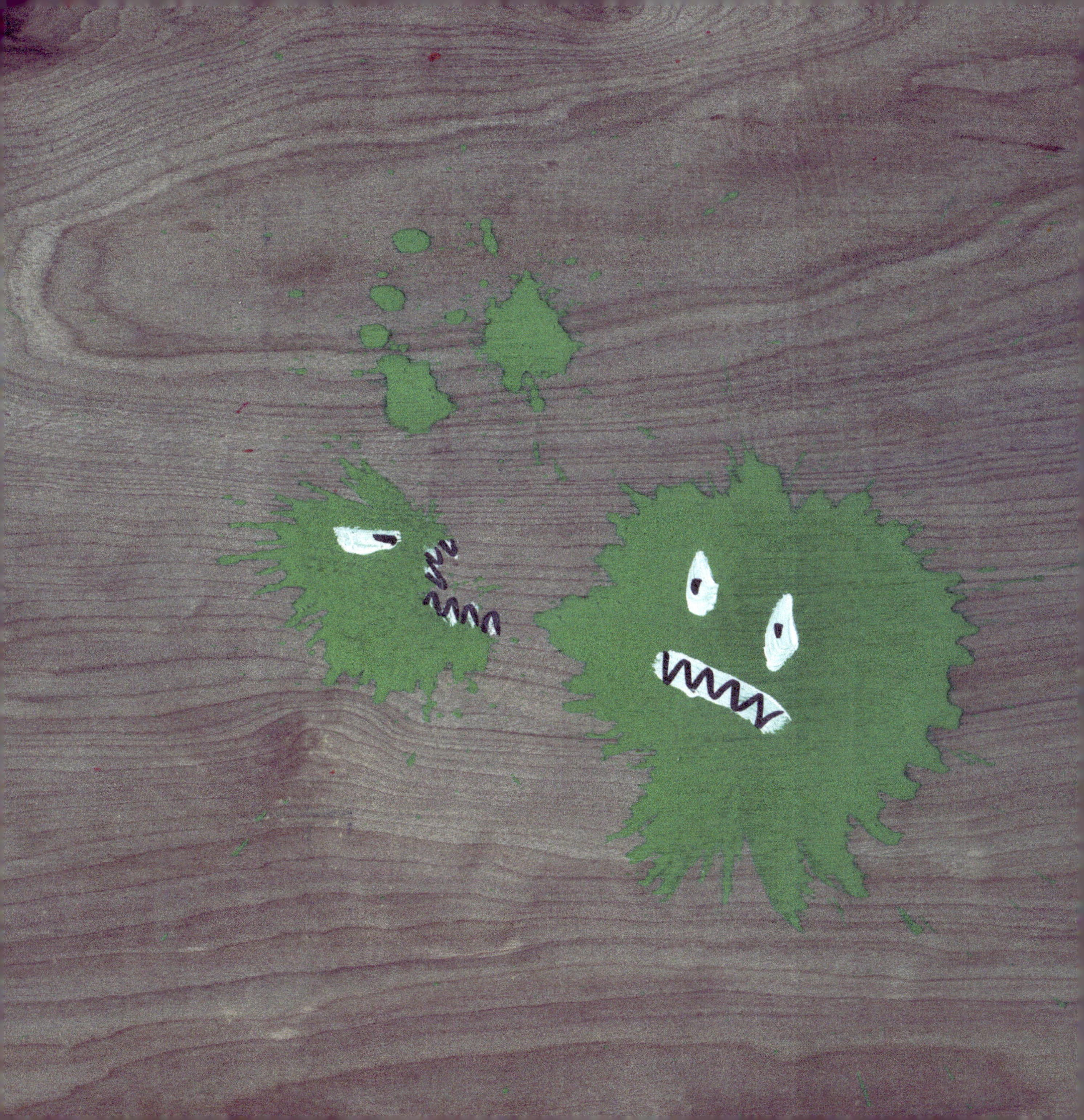

Sacrosanct decisions, derisions, and
Indispensable descriptions
Steady now.
Don't buck so much
They're here to f—
And have a little laugh
And saw a man in half
And slide slide
Slide through haunted images that

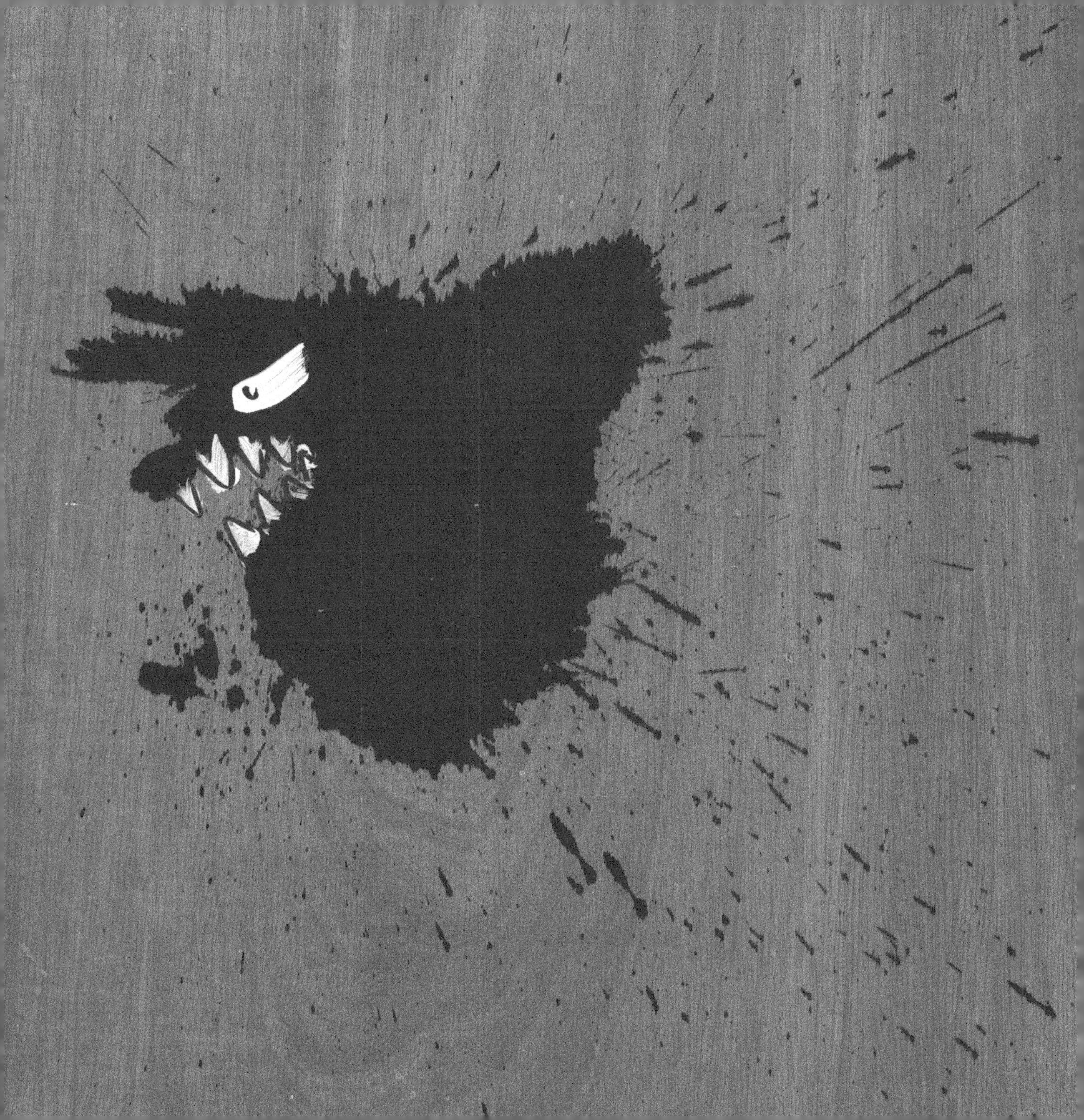

Trouble my visage and
Spoil the view of
Trembling, burrowed you, as they do
Beside the boy you thought you knew
Until until

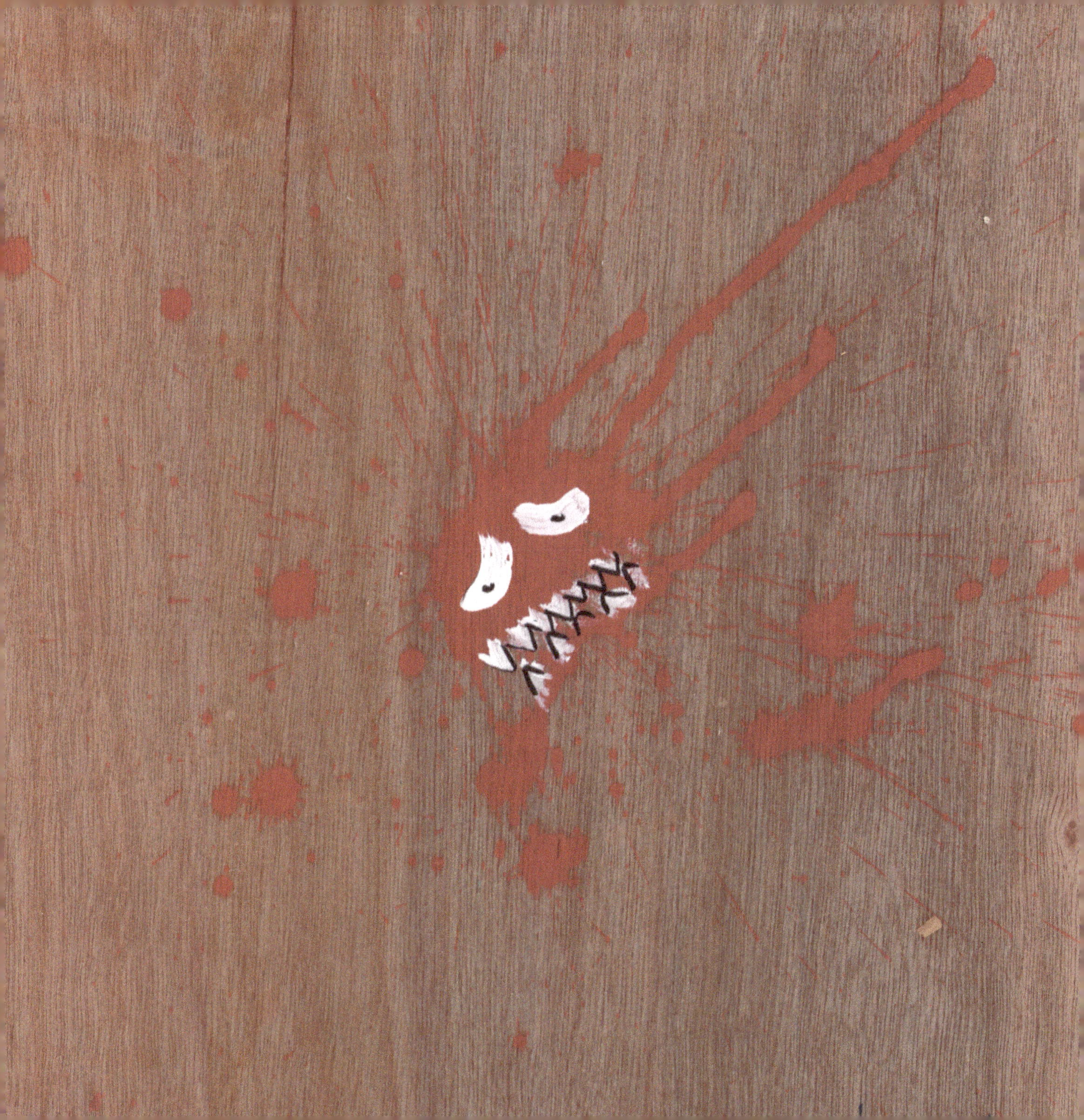

Until you hear me coming through
Up and out as lovers do—
Loud and clear, scream and shout
Transistors fail, over and out

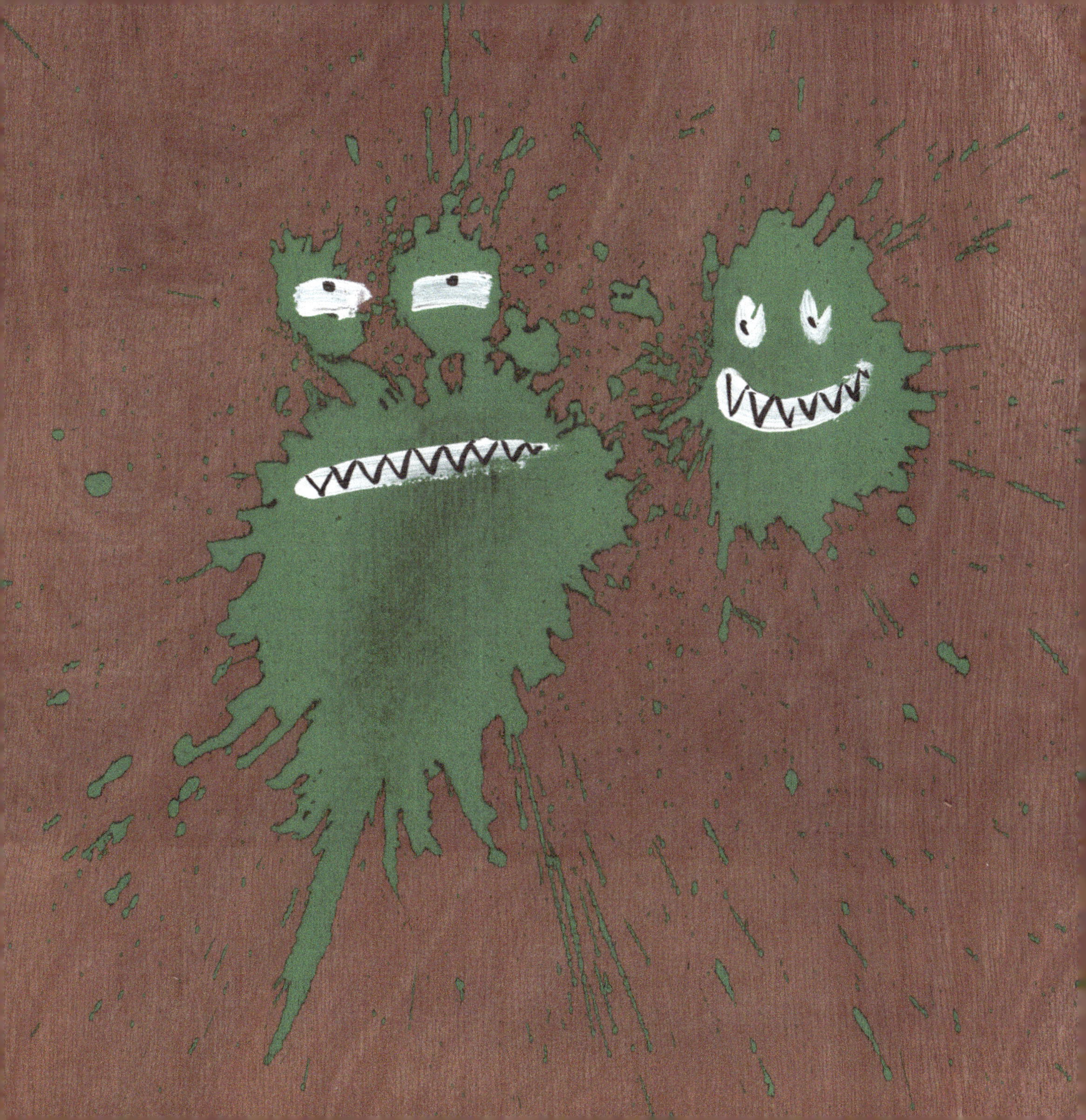

Vacuum tube Valentine

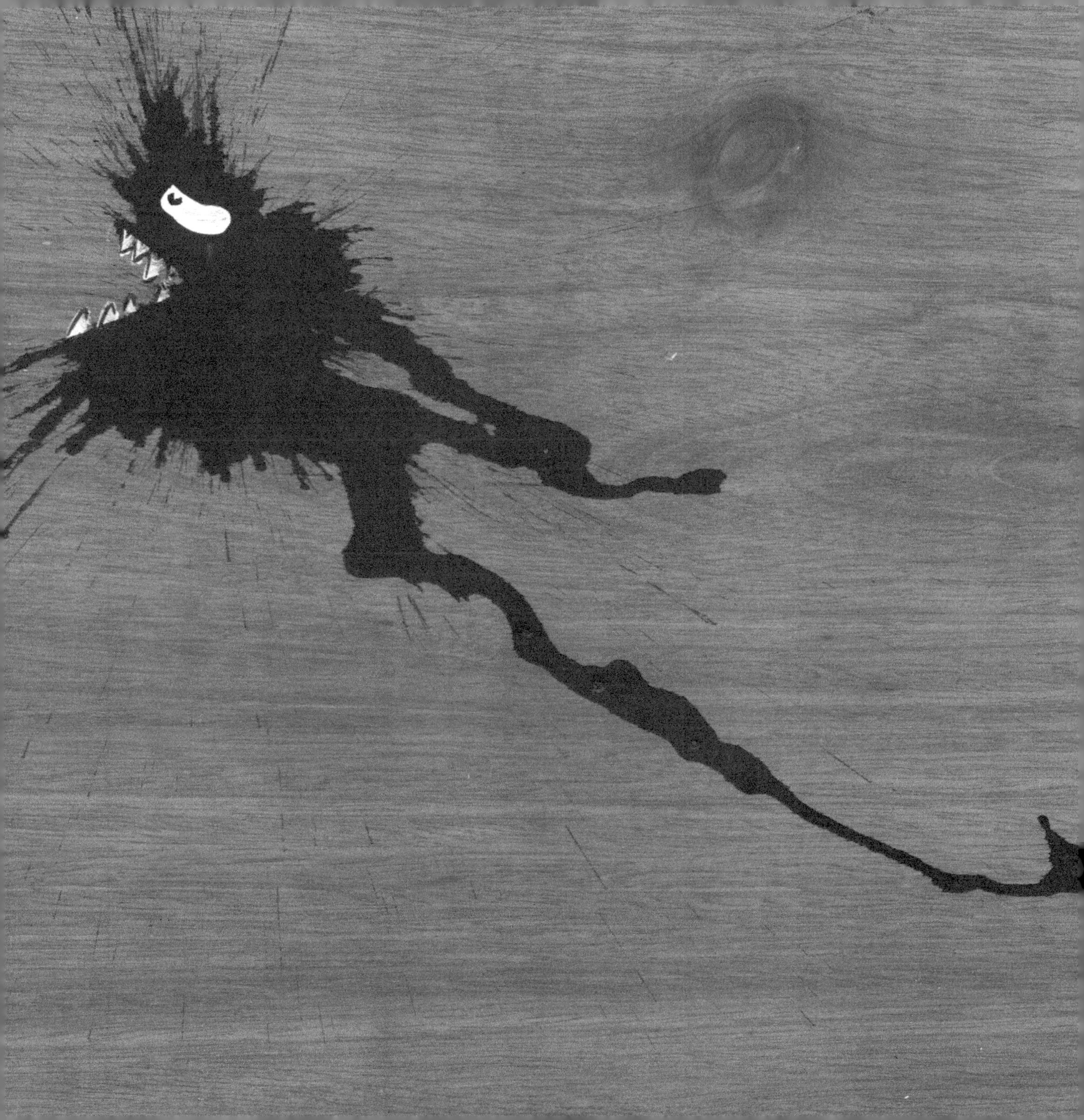

Will you be...
Ellipses
Trail off, or what? He or she
Whispers sad demise and cries
Wanton lusts abide your lies
When time does fail to cut the ties

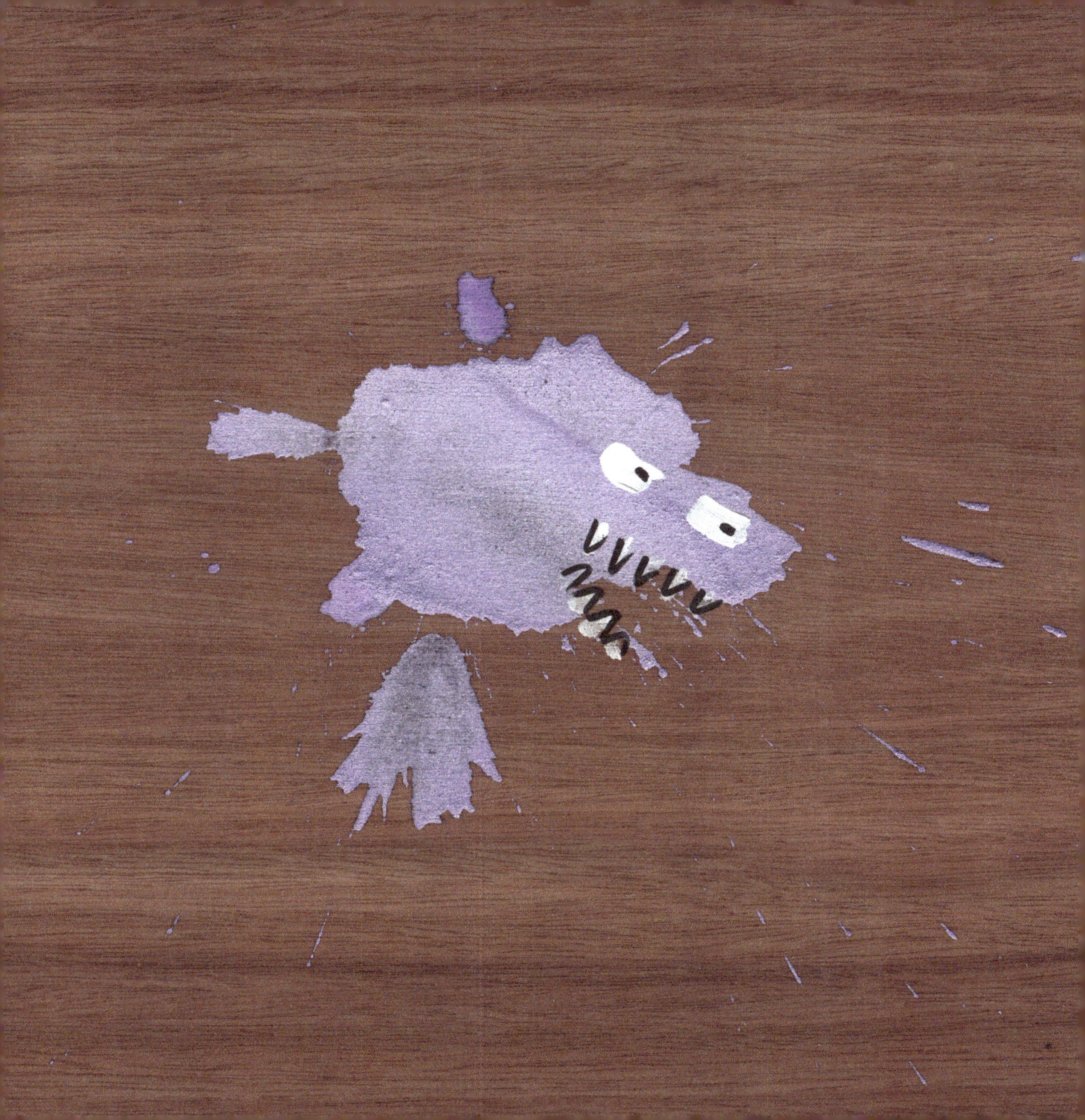

X out their eyes
With markers and clenched fist
And every foul black wish
Unfurled tail and things uncurled and

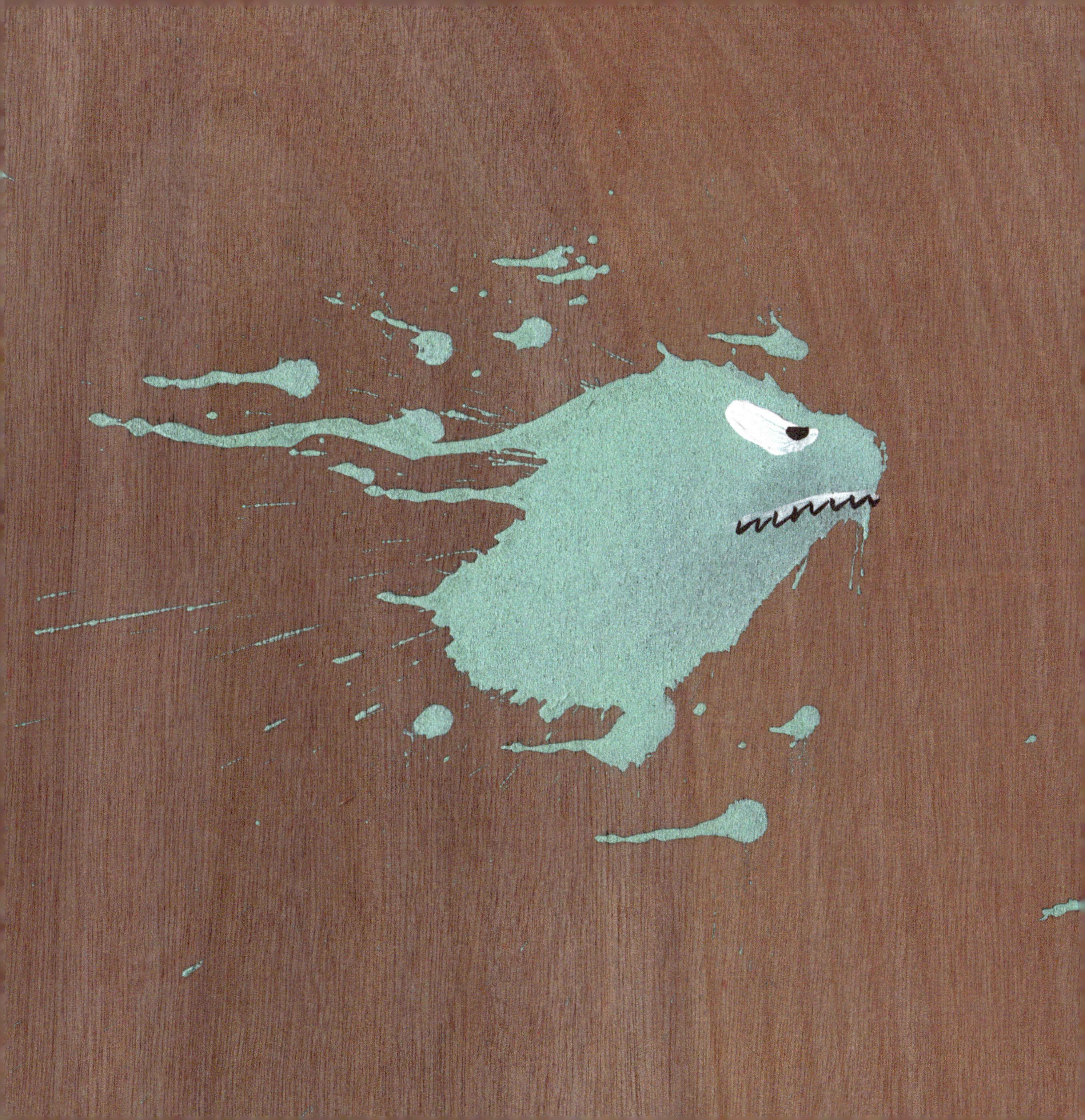

Youthful vision you showed the world
To hide your scales. Your fur. Your glowing eyes.
Fire on your breath, your breasts,
Your charismatic thighs.
You go ahead:
Hide from them if you will
You slide,
I'm hiding still.
But it's too late now as it was too late then

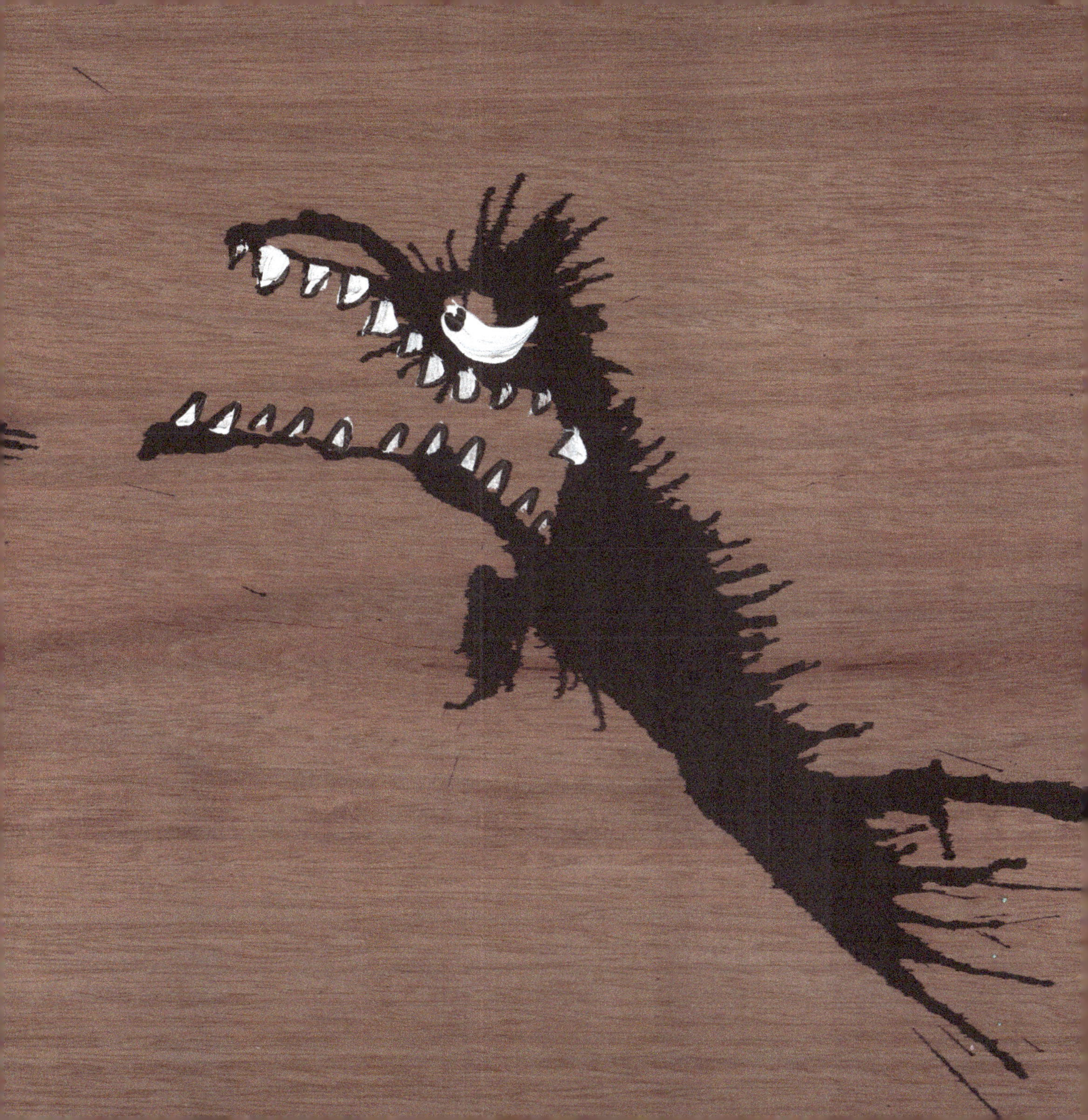

Zero hour for monsters,
Misanthropes,
And men

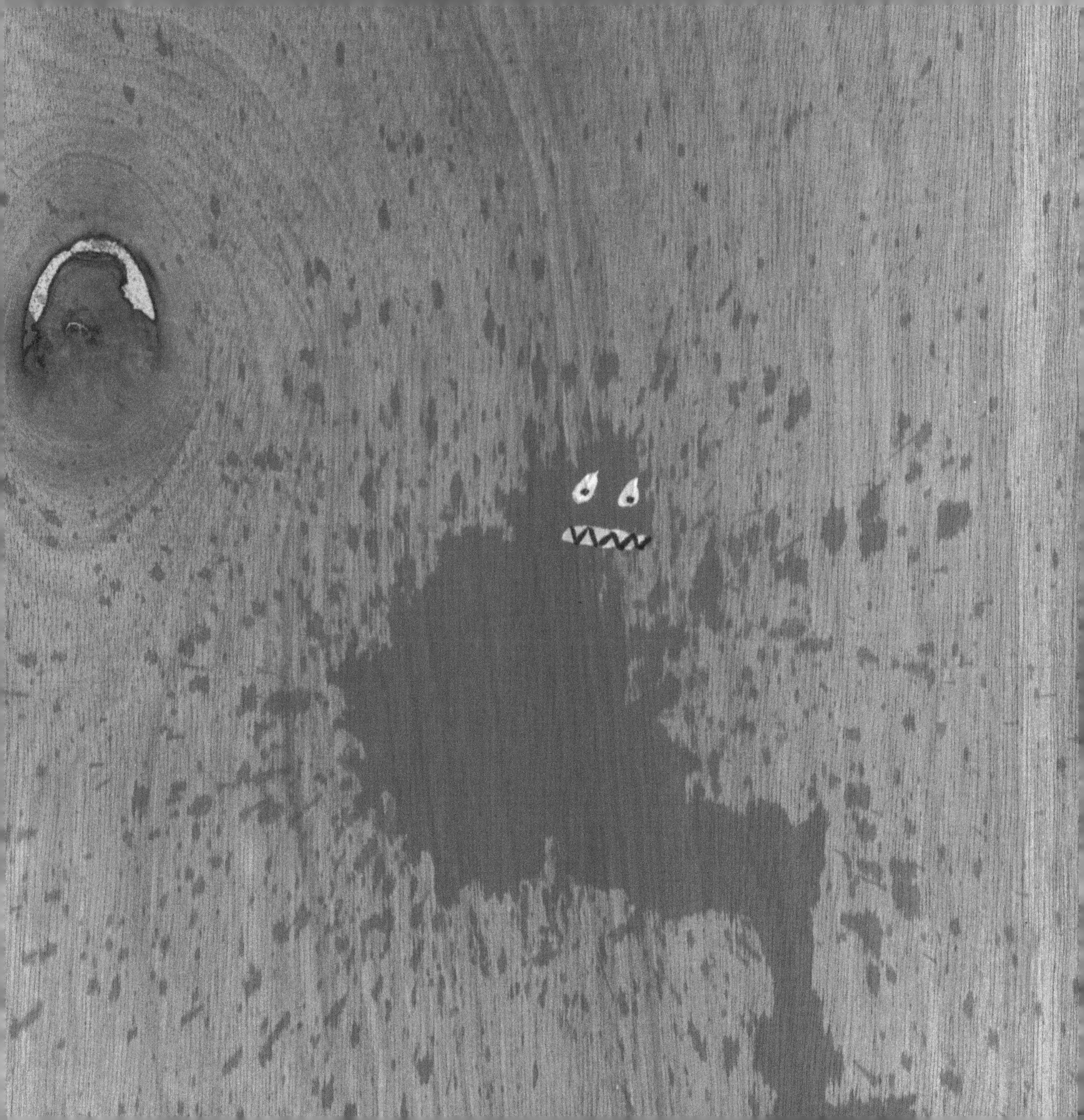

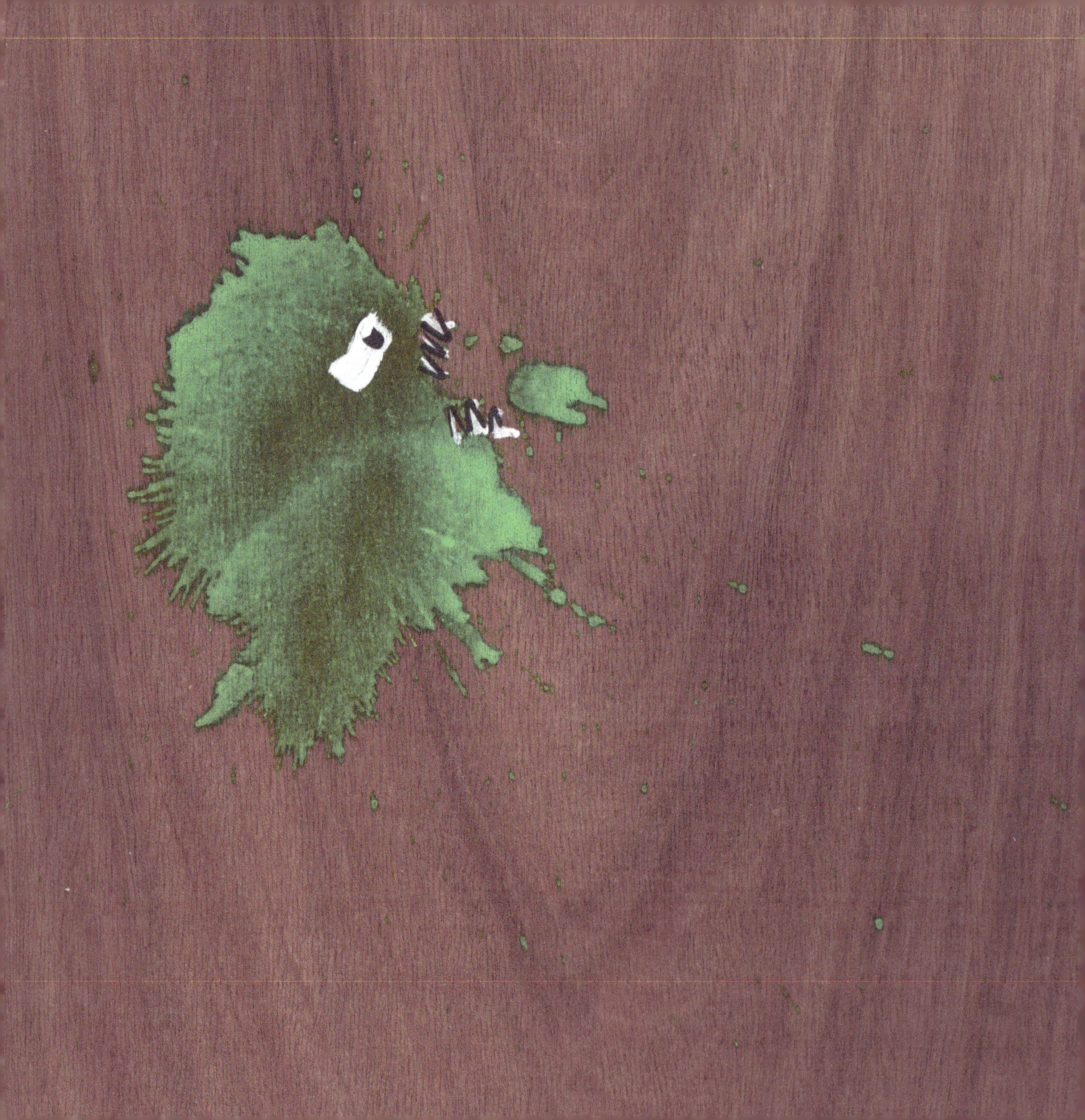

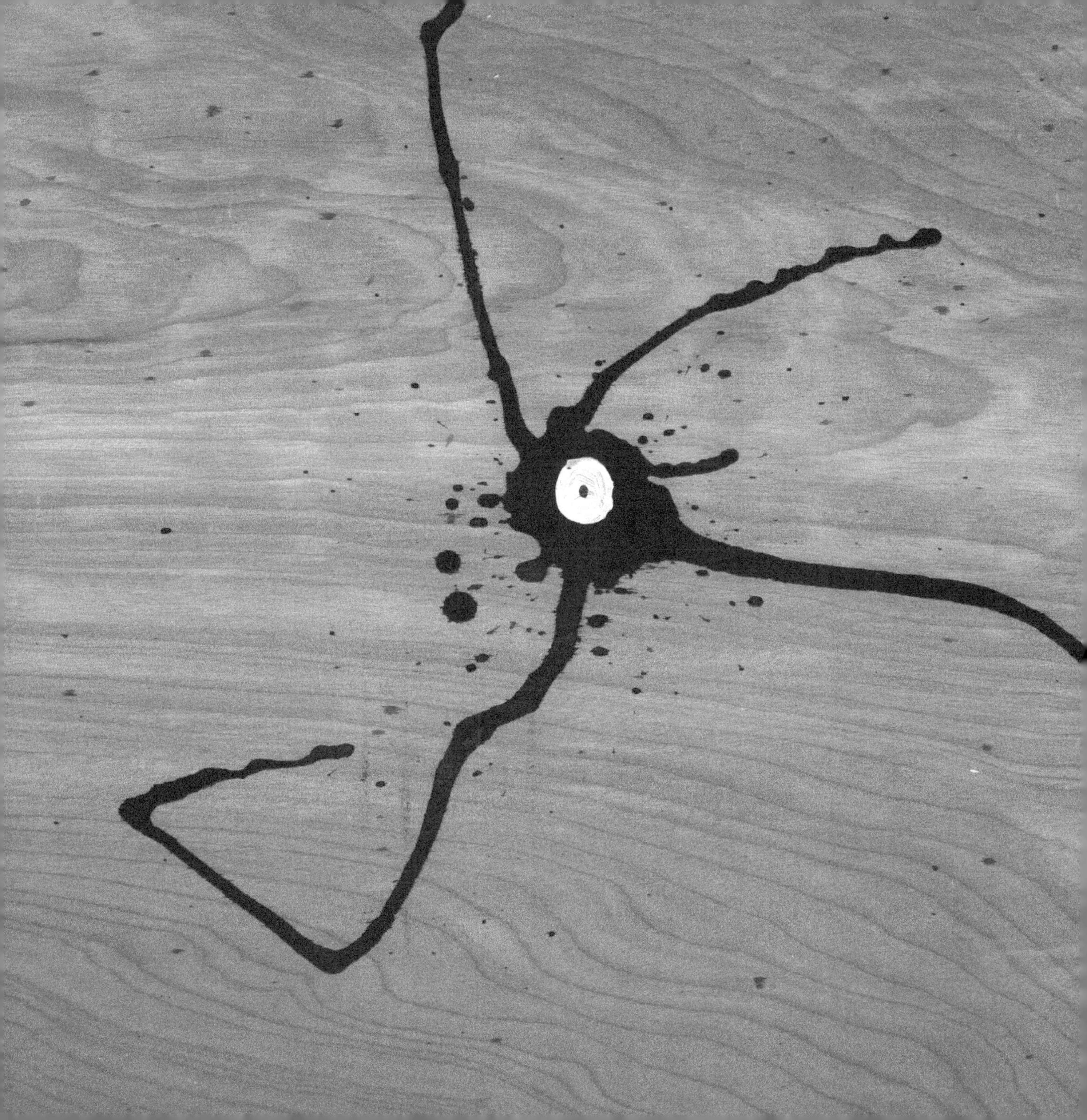

P. Calavara is something like a person or persons living in beautiful Olympia, WA.
They are an enigma, illusions of personification: true stories from a fictional life.
They also do birthday parties. Call for availability.

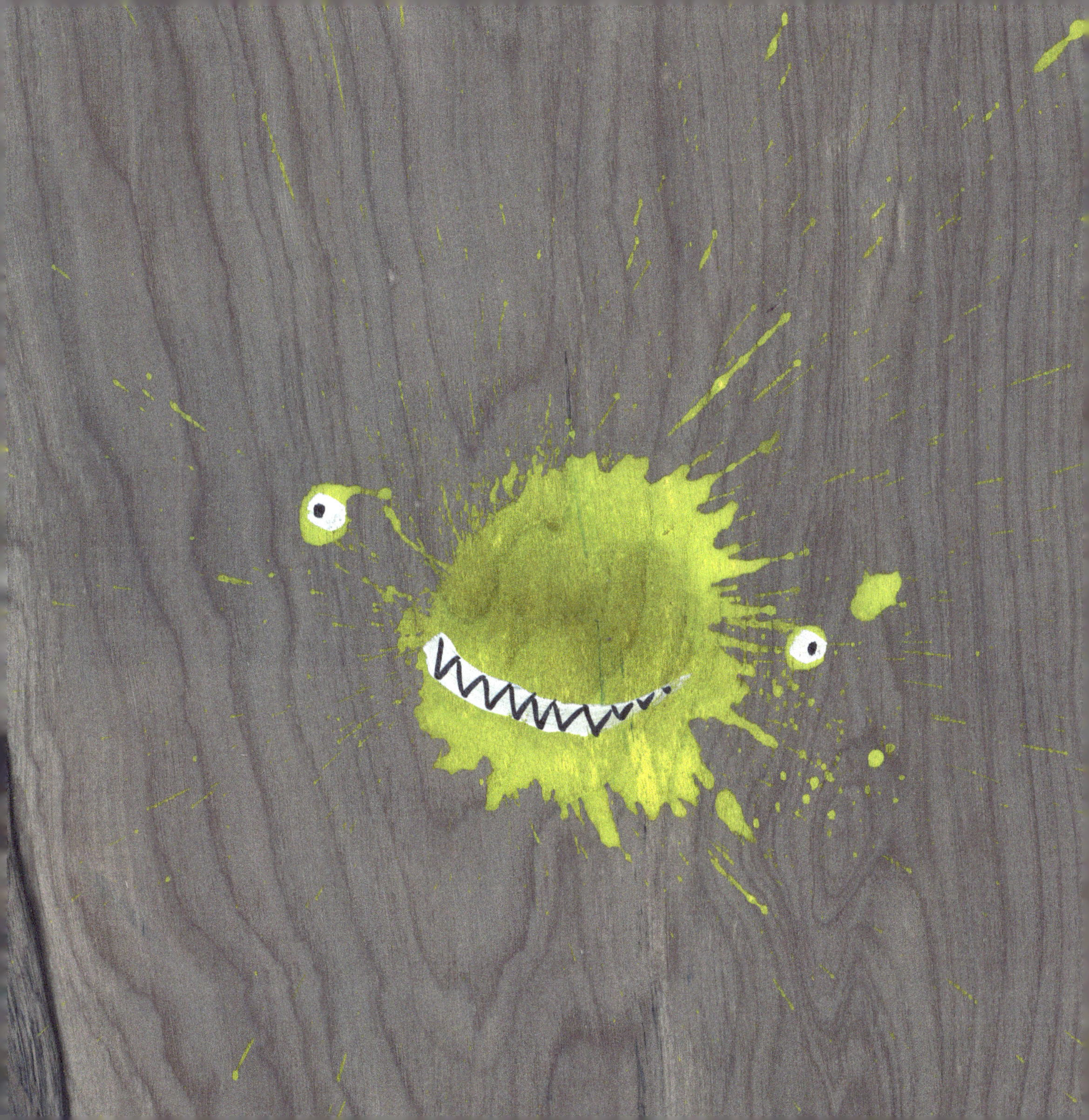

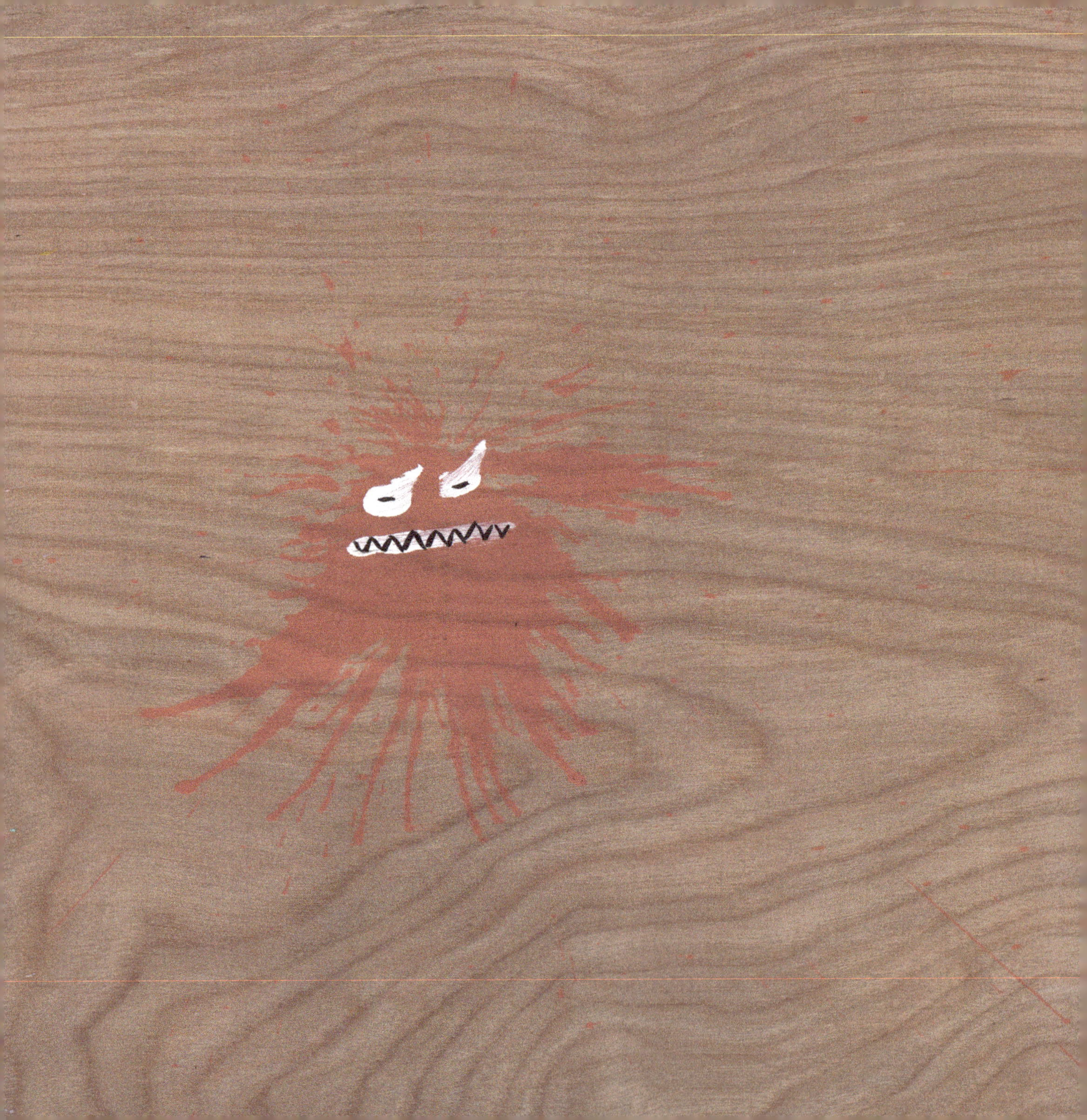

* 9 7 8 0 9 9 9 1 6 4 7 7 5 0 *